Helping People
LEARN
ENGLISH

Helping People
LEARN ENGLISH

A Manual for Teachers of English
as a Second Language

by

Earl W. Stevick

ABINGDON PRESS

NEW YORK   NASHVILLE

HELPING PEOPLE LEARN ENGLISH

Copyright © MCMLV, MCMLVII by Abingdon Press

Library of Congress Catalog Card Number: 57-6121

SET UP, PRINTED, AND BOUND BY THE
PARTHENON PRESS, AT NASHVILLE,
TENNESSEE, UNITED STATES OF AMERICA

FOREWORD

In recent years it has become increasingly apparent that a person who wants to teach a language needs more than a command of the language and an interest in teaching it. The fact that English is one's native tongue does not of itself qualify one to teach it to others.

Yet the United States is undertaking ever-widening responsibilities all over the world. More and more Americans are going out to live in other countries. Inevitably there develops a growing and insistent demand for "untrained native speakers" of English to serve as language tutors, generally on a part-time basis. Some are missionaries. Others are military or diplomatic personnel, or members of their families. Still others are employed by private business concerns.

At the same time, thousands of persons come to this country every year. Some plan to make their homes here and become United States citizens. Others come as college or university students. Almost all need help with the English language. Frequently the teachers who try to give that help are intelligent, dedicated, and in most respects quite competent, but are lacking in acquaintance with the techniques and materials employed by specialists in this work.

We recognize that it would be impracticable to ask all these persons to complete semester courses in teaching English as a second language before they undertake work of this kind. We must further recognize, I believe, that these untrained persons should not be discouraged from trying to help their interested neighbors learn some English. The loss of personal contact and communication would be too great on both sides, both on an individual and on a national level.

However, it is not necessary for such teachers to proceed without any knowledge of the accumulated experience of others. Ideally, as they devote more and more energy to their teaching, they will invest corresponding amounts of time in improving their preparation for the work.

What we have tried to produce, therefore, is a manual which will be brief enough and readable enough for the most casually interested beginner, but which will be useful and sound as far as it goes and will then direct the reader to other, more complete treatments of the same subject matter.

This manual has grown out of attempts to communicate to many groups of students, in as compact a form as possible, the rudiments of teaching English as a foreign language. It is based on personal experience, on reading, and on correspondence with numerous untrained or partially trained teachers abroad.

I should like to express my special thanks to Professor Aileen Traver Kitchin and Mrs. Elizabeth Gillilan Mitchell, under whom I received my grounding in the teaching of English as a foreign language; to the linguists and teachers from many parts of the world who have read

and criticized two earlier versions of this handbook; to Miss
Vivian Morter, who has given the final manuscript a careful reading and has made countless valuable suggestions;
and to the teachers and future teachers in the classes in
which the preliminary drafts have been tested.

Earl W. Stevick

CONTENTS

PART I. Some Fundamental Ideas   13

    1. *What Language Is*   13
    2. *What Language-Learning Is*   14
    3. *What Language-Teaching Is*   18
    4. *An Oral Approach to Language-*
       Learning   23
    5. *Moving Ahead Step by Step*   25

PART II. Teaching Suggestions   29

    1. *Some General Suggestions*   29
       a) You never have to work alone   29
       b) That first class   29
       c) Using "controls"   31
       d) Some suggestions for using
          pictures   34
       e) Routines   39

2. *Teaching Pronunciation*   42

3. *Teaching Grammar*   48

4. *Teaching Vocabulary*   57

5. *Conversation Classes*   60

6. *Reading and Writing*   66

7. *Some Notes on Conversation, Reading, and Writing*   72

8. *What About Audio-Visual Aids?*   74

9. *Other Features of Your Teaching Situation*   78

    a) How old are your students?   78

    b) How much English do your students already know?   81

    c) How often does your class meet? . .   84

    d) What is the size of your class?   84

    e) Is attendance voluntary?   85

    f) Will your students have time for homework?   85

    g) Are you working in an established school?   86

PART III. Some Useful Information About the English Language   87

1. *About the Sounds of English*   87

2. *About English Grammar* 103

    a) Exercises, Set 1 103

    b) Exercises, Set 2 104

    c) Exercises, Set 3 107

    d) Dealing with mistakes in grammar . . 117

PART IV. "What Now?" 124

   Bibliography 127

   Appendix 131

PART I

Some Fundamental Ideas

"My only qualification for teaching English is that I speak it. What teaching I do, I do on the basis of friendship, two nights a week, with a small group of newly arrived housewives here in Connecticut. Our textbook is _____ _____, but mostly we just do the best we can."

"I am supposed to teach oral English here in Malaya to a group of forty boys, twelve to fifteen years of age. They have had English all through their school . . ."

"My friends here keep asking me to give them English lessons, but I really don't know how to begin. . . ."

Three part-time teachers, teaching English as a foreign language. Which of them has most in common with you?

Before we talk about "you as a teacher," let's take a look at "you as a learner" of English.

1. *What Language Is*

As you were growing up, you learned to behave in certain ways in certain situations. You learned to feed yourself —in a certain way. You learned to tie your shoes, probably with a bowknot. You learned how to conduct yourself in school, how to get along with other children, how to behave when being introduced to an adult. We all learned these ways of behaving, and learned them so thoroughly that other ways of doing these same things seem strange to us, if not wrong or downright incredible.

Along with ways of acting, you learned to produce and respond to a set of symbols which consisted of noises. These symbols accompanied and stood for various phases of life as you were experiencing it. Most of these symbols were made by using lips, tongue, voice box, and the like.

As a matter of fact, these symbols were of many kinds. There were vowels and consonants, of course, but also voice pitches and different degrees of loudness. You chose different words, but you also put endings on some of them, or put the same words now in one order, now in another. And all of these signaling devices meshed together in a quite remarkable way, forming an unbelievably complex system. As the years went by and the system worked itself deeper and deeper into the set of habits by which you lived, you learned to call that system "the English language."

2. *What Language-Learning Is*

Fortunately, we were allowed to learn this system a little at a time. We had other advantages, too, that kept us from being overwhelmed. We learned from the loving help of parents, as well as from the ridicule of playmates who gave us no peace until we talked "like everybody else." We "studied the language" every waking hour. But now let's turn our attention to the person who learns a new language after he has thoroughly mastered his mother tongue.

Here are two descriptions of what it means to have "learned a foreign language":

14

a) A person has learned a foreign language when he has
... first, within a limited vocabulary, mastered the sound system
(that is, when he can understand the stream of speech and
achieve an understandable production of it) and has, second,
made the structural devices (that is, the basic arrangements of
utterances) matters of automatic habit.[1]

b) A person has learned a foreign language when he is
able to understand and use understandably the expressions he
needs in any situation in which he participates. He has partially
learned a foreign language when he can use and understand
part of the expressions which he needs.

That is, in the situation "asking one's way on the street,"
one needs to *use* such expressions as:

(*List A*)

> Pardon me.
> Where's the post office?
> Thank you.
> Well, thanks just the same.

One also need to *understand* expressions like:

(*List B*)

> It's on Main Street, two blocks up that way.
> I don't know. I'm a stranger here myself.
> You're quite welcome.
> Sorry.

In the situation "small talk at a tea or reception," on the
other hand, one uses and responds to a quite different set
of expressions. Some of them are:

[1] Fries, C. C., *Teaching and Learning English as a Foreign Language*, p. 3.

15

(*List C*)

> Good evening.
> Where's your home?
> It's in Canada.
> How interesting!
> Are you a stranger here?
> Yes, this is the first time I've been here.

No expression appears on any two of these three lists, yet there is more or less carry-over from the expressions you learn for one situation to the expressions you have to learn for another. For instance, "where's" occurs in Lists A and C, while "it's" occurs in B and C. The word "the" is found in A and C; "stranger" and "here" are shared by B and C. Less conspicuous but just as important, the three lists draw on the same stock of vowels and consonants and use the same basic "sentence melodies." The trick for the learner is to take advantage of this carry-over with the least possible fuss and confusion.

Now let's compare our two descriptions of language learning (p. 15). The first talks about vocabulary, sound system, and structural devices, whereas the second talks about whole expressions in larger conversational wholes. The two are closely related, for the carry-over referred to in Description 2*b* is most easily statable in the linguistic terms of the former definition.

One more thing that you need to remember about Description 2*b*: as you go from country to country, and culture to culture, you will expect to find differences in *how* people say things. But you must also expect to find differences between your students' languages and English with respect to *what* they say in different situations. Most important, and most difficult of all, you must remember

16

that *the situations themselves differ* from culture to culture. You can see this most easily in the physical objects that you encounter in various countries. The situation in which you offer someone a mango does not occur in places where mangoes are unknown. Sometimes, however, the differences are less obvious.

For example, in one language there is an expression which corresponds rather closely to our "thank you." Yet if someone says "thank you" to you in this language, you do not ordinarily respond in words. That is, this language has no expression that functions quite like our "you're welcome."

An even greater difference is found in the simple matter of how two people greet each other in the morning. In English the following exchanges are considered quite adequate and courteous:

> A: Good morning!
> B: Good morning!

> or

> A: Good morning! How are you today?
> B: Fine. How're you?
> A: Fine.

On the other hand, in at least one language of the world such brevity would be rude. A typical morning exchange, translated literally, goes something like this:

> A: It is morning.
> B: It is morning. Did you sleep?
> A: I slept if you slept.
> B: Yes, I slept.
> A: Did your father and mother sleep?

17

B: Yes, they slept.
A: Did your wife and children . . . (etc.).

Learning a language, then, includes becoming familiar with the situations in which the speakers of the language ordinarily use it, as well as with the sounds, words, and grammatical system.

3. *What Language-Teaching Is*

The details of your job as a teacher of English will vary greatly, depending on the number, ages, and backgrounds of the people you teach. We will have more to say about these details in Part II. In this section we are merely pointing out some things you will need to remember, no matter what kind of class you have.

Some people like to say that there is no such thing as language-teaching: "Languages cannot be taught; they must be learned." Even if that is true, there are still certain things that you can do to help your students learn English:

a) Give them a reliable model to imitate. In a reading class this means choosing books that contain the kind of English your students are going to need in the future. Almost all students will need stories which provide practice with everyday English. Students who are further advanced and who are going into the business world will want to practice on books and articles that have to do with industry, finance, and so forth. Others will want to become familiar with the language of Emerson, Swift, Milton, or Shakespeare. Still others will have other interests.

But it is for the spoken language that the teacher is really indispensable as a model. Your student cannot learn English pronunciation from a book. Even if he has access to a set of recordings, he needs someone who can point

18

out where his imitation is faulty. And that someone must be willing to point out the same mistakes over and over again, patiently and constructively.

One thing that many people don't realize: if English is your native language, you shouldn't worry about speaking with an "accent." Whether you are from Georgia, Massachusetts, Edinburgh, or New Zealand, your form of English is adequate to make you understood all over the English-speaking world. It is much better for your student if he imitates *you* than if he first listens to you and then tries to apply a series of "corrections" to what he hears— artificial corrections that neither he nor you really understands.

Finally, don't forget to supply a model for the culture as well as for the language. As students become more advanced, it is appropriate to give them an idea of some of the situations which are common in our culture, but which may be quite foreign to them. For example, you can tell your students some of your own experiences. You can have them listen to radio broadcasts, read stories and articles, or correspond with "pen pals" in the English-speaking world. Or you can help them interpret pictures like the ones found on the covers of the *Saturday Evening Post*.

b) *Keep your students from becoming confused.* The art of making explanations and answering questions about a foreign language is a difficult one. There is no substitute for thorough training, for reading what linguists have written about English, and for long hours spent trying to work out explanations that are at the same time clear, accurate, and comprehensive.[2]

[2] You can get some help from Part III of this manual, but we urge you to go on to such works as Fries, *op. cit.*; Fries' *Structure*

19

Meantime, here are a few rules of thumb that may help you in this delicate business of answering questions and making explanations:

(1) *Don't even try to answer questions that begin with the word "why."* Suppose someone asks you "why" you said "I'd like some coffee," but "I don't want any tea, thank you." He'll ask, "Why did you use 'some' in one sentence and 'any' in the other?" Or perhaps, "Why did you use 'would like' in one sentence and 'don't want' in the other? Don't 'wouldn't like' and 'don't want' mean the same thing?" These are typical of the questions you meet when you are teaching English as a foreign language.

If you try to answer such "why"-questions directly, in terms of how the speaker "feels" or what he "means" when he uses one form or the other, you are almost certain to be confusing. It's better to rephrase the question, either aloud or to yourself. Ask a similar question that begins with "when," or "where," or "under what circumstances." Then try to answer in objective terms which allow no room for misunderstanding.

The question about "some" and "any" for instance, might become "When do you use 'some,' and when 'any'?" A partial answer, applicable to the sentences that prompted this question, would then be, "In questions, use 'some' or 'any'; in statements after a negative, use 'any'; in other statements, use 'some.'"

The question about "would like" and "don't want"

---

of English; the journals *Language Learning* and *English Language Teaching*; Hornby, *A Guide to Patterns and Usage in English.* You will also find much of value in the notes and comments included in: Fries, *et al., Intensive Course in English;* and Agard, *et al., El Inglés Hablado.* For your convenience, the grammatical notes contained in large parts of the latter two works are indexed in the Appendix.

could be rephrased in a similar way. This time, however, the answer is even more complex. When, as in this instance, you can't state an answer in simple, objective terms, you can still help your students in three important ways: (a) you can assure them that "we really do say it that way"; (b) you can supply some other, similar sentences: "Would you like to ride?" "I don't want to go." "I'd like some sugar." "I don't want any money." "I'd like a ticket, please." Finally, (c) you can try to refrain from saying any more about it. If you succeed, you will save time and avoid confusion.

(2) *Stick close to the sentence or sentences that are causing the problem;* don't generalize beyond the evidence at hand.

For example, we have in English the "present" forms:

> I want it.
> I do want it.

Now, you're perfectly safe if you tell your student that the difference between *these two* sentences is that the second is more emphatic than the first. But if you tell your students that the verb phrase with the auxiliary "do" is always emphatic, he will completely misinterpret casual questions like:

> Do you want it?

c) *Help your students stay interested.* Learning a new language is a long, hard process, no matter how bright the student or how skillful the teacher. If a student gets bored, he may stop his study of English altogether. Even if he doesn't stop *studying,* he will soon stop *learning* English.

(1) *Be cheerful with your students.* Give them a chance to laugh whenever you can. What they've laughed at, they'll remember.

Just one caution: what you have learned to consider funny may seem unfunny to your students. In their culture it may be pointless, rude, or even obscene. There is no substitute for an intimate knowledge of your students' ways of living and thinking.

(2) *Be careful how you correct students' mistakes. Don't* ridicule them. *Don't* be sarcastic. *Don't* scold. These three "don'ts" apply no matter where you are, of course, but they're incomparably more important among peoples who are very concerned with "keeping face."

Then how can you correct mistakes without making people "lose face"? You will discover an answer to this question only as you yourself become a member of the local culture and find out how your people do things.

In the meantime, though, "accentuate the positive." Encourage your students to mimic you, praise good mimicry, and don't feel that you have to correct every mistake the moment it is made.

(3) *Mind your manners.* This means your manners as interpreted by your students. A good friend of mine once started English classes as part of his missionary assignment. At first he had more students than he could handle. Soon, however, attendance began to drop rapidly for no apparent reason. Finally someone explained the reason to him. He had been pointing at the boy or girl that he wanted to call on. But the pupils had been brought up to consider such a gesture highly offensive.

(4) *Save your creative ideas for the big problems; relegate classroom details to a set of routines.* Work is more

pleasant and more efficient when both you and your students know what the class is to do next.

Not long ago I had an opportunity to observe a hundred hours of classes in elementary French, German, and Spanish. The classes were taught by over twenty different people. Often I watched two or three teachers teach the same lesson material. The best teachers were able to give their students three times as much practice as the poor ones could. Moreover, their students enjoyed their classwork more, and seemed no more fatigued at the end of the hour than did the students in classes taught by the poorer teachers. How were the better teachers able to do this?

They did it by establishing *and maintaining* a set of routines. The students had learned these routines during the first week they were with their instructors. The class proceeded smoothly from start to finish. (For an example of what may happen if you don't establish an efficient set of routines, see pp. 40-41.)

4. *An Oral Approach to Language-Learning*

You've probably heard language teachers talking about the different "methods" of language study: "the direct method," "the reading method," "my own method," and so forth.[3] In this manual we occasionally refer to or give

[3] For a collection of articles on methods and techniques, see Newmark, *Twentieth Century Modern Language Teaching,* Ch. 6. See also the many articles in the journals *Language Learning* and *English Language Teaching,* and the short summaries of various methodologies in Anne Cochran's *Modern Methods of Teaching English as a Foreign Language.* Palmer's *The Teaching of Oral English* contains many specific devices for direct-method teaching. Jespersen's *How to Teach a Foreign Language* is particularly rich in methods for use with the secondary school pupils. Gurrey's *Teaching English as a Foreign Language* is another valuable source.

samples of one method or another. But our purpose is not to propagate a method or to suggest a single set of materials, used according to an invariable set of procedures.

Our aim is to set forth an approach to problems of teaching and learning languages. We call this "the oral approach." [4] We believe that it can lead to smoother, more efficient learning—to a higher return on the many hours of hard work that language mastery requires.

As its name suggests, the "oral approach" is based on the assumption that the spoken language underlies writing, and not vice versa. The approach has been summarized: "Hearing before speaking, speaking before reading, reading before writing."

Speech, of course, is a physical activity carried on—like other physical activities—by muscles. The muscles most conspicuously involved are those of the tongue, jaw, lips, and diaphragm; but there are many others. If we are to speak at all fluently, the work of these muscles must be governed by a set of habits. The more fluent we want to be, the stronger these habits must become; in one's native language, where fluency is greatest, these habits are almost unbreakable.

For this reason teachers who follow the oral approach hold that language-learning should consist, especially in the first stages, of oral practice; and that the student should do so much oral practice that he can say the sentences he has practiced almost in his sleep, not just in class. While he is practicing, of course, the student should continually have in mind the *meaning* of what he is repeating.

The first important principle of the oral approach, then,

[4] A term used, for example, by Fries in *Teaching and Learning English as a Foreign Language,* and by J. O. Gauntlett in *Basic Principles of English Language Teaching.*

is found at the heart of the little summary quoted above: "speaking before reading." People sometimes misunderstand this central emphasis of the oral approach by regarding it as a prohibition on the use of reading and writing during the first weeks or months of language study. But the oral approach implies no such prohibition. Writing and printed materials can be highly useful. Indeed, without them the load on the student's memory might become intolerable after the first few hours of oral study. What the oral approach does emphasize is that the student should come into contact with the spoken form before he sees the written form, and that ability to decipher and reproduce the written forms should not be confused with language mastery.

A second fundamental principle of the oral approach is expressed by placing "speaking" after "hearing," and "writing" after "reading"; in all that he does, your student should have a clear-cut model to follow. Language-learning, whether by infants or adults, is first of all a matter of imitation. Only as the learner progresses further does he become able to form new expressions that are acceptable to the established speakers of the language; the learner forms these new expressions *only by analogy*—analogy based on the forms he has already learned through imitation. It is quite a problem to know how to help your student progress from straight mimicry to the freedom in analogical creation which you as a native speaker possess. This problem will be the subject of our next section.

5. *Moving Ahead Step by Step*

We have just mentioned the problem of helping the student progress from straight imitation to free conversa-

25

77128

tion or composition. One way in which we can meet this problem is by placing restrictions on what we let the student try to do. These restrictions, or "controls," restrain the student from trying to do too much too soon—from getting in over his head and floundering. As the student grows more proficient, we relax our controls one by one. In this way we hope to minimize frustration and, insofar as possible, keep the student from making errors. Remember that whenever your student *makes* a mistake, he is *practicing* one. In Part II we will discuss specific ways in which you may devise cautious, effective controls of this sort for your students.

In another sense, we need controls on ourselves as teachers, and particularly on the lesson materials which we use. In controlling the content of lesson materials, our aim is to allow our students to meet new difficulties one at a time. We may sort out difficult points fairly satisfactorily into four categories: phonological, grammatical, lexical, and cultural. Phonological difficulties are those relating to the formation and interpretation of sounds. Grammar has to do with the forms and arrangements of words. Lexical problems are problems of vocabulary. Cultural problems and difficulties arise because speakers of Language A differ from speakers of Language B not only in the way they talk, but also in the way they live and in the way they look at the world.

Experience has shown us that what is hard for a speaker of Spanish sometimes presents no difficulty to a speaker of German, or vice versa; a point which is almost impossible for a Russian may seem obvious to an Armenian. For this reason it is well for a set of lessons to take into account not

26

only the structure of the language being taught (say English), but also the structure of the native language of the prospective students.

Once a textbook writer knows which language he is to teach, and to whom, he can determine what his readers' most serious difficulties are going to be. Having discovered which points are going to be hardest, he must decide whether to introduce them at random or in a planned sequence. Thus, some textbooks are written in such a way that no word is used until it has been taught and practiced thoroughly. Other books place less emphasis on vocabulary control but are careful to use no grammatical patterns except those that have been introduced explicitly and drilled at some length. Other materials, combining these two types of control, give more weight to one or the other. Still others place no systematic restrictions on new material.

Because they introduce new difficulties[5] at a manageable rate, carefully sequenced materials can be a great boon to teacher and students alike. A full set of carefully sequenced materials represents a tremendous investment of time and care—much greater than an individual teacher can make. For this reason they are not lightly to be disregarded or departed from. In Part II, 5, we will have more to say concerning sequenced materials.

As for controlling the cultural content of lessons, it is obvious that one would not ask beginning students in the villages of India or the mountains of South America to use lessons which were meaningless to anyone who lacked firsthand knowledge of life in a small American city. One has to "start where the students are." They should not have

_____
[5] Or at least new difficulties of certain kinds.

27

to cope both with new language *and* with new culture at the beginning of their work. But as time goes on, the content of the lessons may shift gradually until it embraces features of English-speaking culture quite foreign to the students' direct experience.

PART II

Teaching Suggestions

1. *Some General Suggestions*

a) You never have to work alone. This handbook is written for the nonprofessional teacher. Likely as not, if you are a nonprofessional teacher, you are working pretty much alone. Here is one general caution before we start discussing specific problems: don't be any more alone than you have to be. Look around for whatever help is available. For example, if you are teaching overseas, the local office of the United States Information Service or of the British Council may be able to give invaluable help.

By reading, too, you can keep from being "alone" in your teaching. We hope you will read what is in this handbook and work out for yourself the exercises in Part III. But don't stop there! After you've finished this manual, go on to more comprehensive works, such as those in the bibliography on pp. 127-30.

b) That first class. This section is for you if your total experience teaching English as a foreign language is nearly —or exactly—zero. "Suppose they don't understand me?" "Suppose I discourage them by giving them work that is too hard?" "What if I insult them by giving them something too easy?" "I hope they don't ask any questions I can't answer!"

Since classes are of so many kinds, we can't recommend

some single technique especially for "first classes." About all we can do is give you some "memory verses" to fall back on —and on which many others before you have fallen back. Part of your students' success depends on their confidence in you. For this reason, if you come to the beginning of the hour—or the middle of it—unsure of what you are going to do next, try not to let your students know it. You will be less likely to run into this problem if you:

(1) Plan your first class in great detail. List the aims of the hour and the exact steps by which you expect to achieve those aims.

(2) Establish rapport with the group during the first hour; also begin getting acquainted with its members—by name if possible.

(3) Plan to have a large number of times in that hour when you can pause, smile, and say, "Yes, that's it," or its equivalent. In other words, be sure your students leave with a feeling of accomplishment. If they do, you will!

(4) Give them a lesson that's too easy rather than one that's too hard.

(5) Finally, don't worry too much if you don't speak their language and they don't speak English. After all, people have communicated across language boundaries for thousands and thousands of years. Given a little patience and a sense of humor on both sides, you can soon teach your students what English you need for conducting the class, and then you're ready to go head! As you probably know, the "direct" method refuses to use the student's language even when it is available. Handy sources of ideas in this situation are Palmer's *Teaching of Oral English* and the pocket book *English Through Pictures* by Richards and Gibson.

c) Using "controls": On p. 26 we said that you as teacher should try to prevent your students from attempting too much too soon. We also said that, as they grow surer of themselves, you should give them greater freedom. Any techniques that you use to achieve these two aims, we call "controls."

We have worked out the control principle concretely in connection with a series of leaflets, one of which is reproduced on pp. 32-33. Here are some comments on it:

Basic selection: Students should hear the story a few times before they receive the leaflets. Control is complete in that students have no chance to make mistakes as yet. After two or three readings students may ask for repetitions of parts or for explanations. Control is close, since the range of questions that the students will use will be narrow: "What does ——— mean?" and so forth. The miniature glossary at the foot of the basic selection may be of some help.

"Yes"-"no" questions: Control is still close, since all the student has to do is remember the story, understand the question (which uses words from the story), and choose the right answer: "yes" or "no." Or you may require him to choose the right pronoun and the right verb for such answers as "Yes, he does," "No, it isn't." You can tighten control here by giving the appropriate sentence from the story just before you ask each question.

Other questions: These questions represent a relaxation of controls because now the student must choose from a wider range of possible answers and must use words not contained in the question.

Similar sentences: The purpose of this section is first to highlight certain grammatical points and then to let students practice them. Number 1, for example, gives prac-

31

Basic Selection:

A man named Nathan Beck lives in Columbus, Ohio. Columbus has a population of over 374,000.

One day not long ago, the postman delivered a letter to Mr. Beck. The words "Columbus, Ohio" were written at the bottom of the envelope, and there was a stamp in the upper right-hand corner. But Beck's name was not on the letter. The street address was missing, too. In place of the name and street address, there was a photograph of Beck on the outside of the envelope.

Beck opened the envelope. Inside he found a letter from a friend of his in California. The letter said, "I just wanted to see if you really were a big shot in your home town."

It was *missing* from the envelope—it should have been on the envelope, but it was not there.

He's a "big shot"—He's an important person (slang).

Columbus is his *home town*—His permanent home is in Columbus.

"Yes"-"No" Questions (give short answers):

1. Does Mr. Beck live in Columbus, Ohio?
2. Does Mr. Beck live in Columbus, Georgia?
3. Has Columbus a population of over 374,000?
4. Is Columbus a small town?
5. Did the postman deliver a letter to Beck?
6. Did he deliver a package to Beck?
7. Were the words "Columbus, Ohio" written at the bottom of the envelope?
8. Was there a stamp on the envelope?
9. Was Beck's name on the envelope?
10. Was Beck's street address on the envelope?
11. Was there a photograph on the outside of the envelope?
12. Did Beck open the envelope?
13. Was there a letter in the envelope?
14. Was the letter from a friend of Beck's?
15. Was Beck really a "big shot" in Columbus?

Other Questions (give short answers):

1. Where does Mr. Beck live?
2. How large is Columbus?
3. Who delivered a letter to Beck?
4. What did the postman deliver to Beck?
5. What was on the envelope?
6. What was missing from the envelope?
7. Where was the photograph?
8. Who was it a photograph of?
9. What did Mr. Beck do with the envelope?
10. Who was the letter from?
11. What did the letter say?
12. Why did Mr. Beck's friend send the letter?

1. Columbus has a population of over 374,000.
   Nashville —173,000
   Denver —412,000
   Memphis —394,000
   St. Louis —852,000
   Cleveland —905,000

2. Where is the upper-right hand (lower left-hand) corner of the envelope?

3. The words were in the upper right-hand (lower left-hand) corner.

4. The words were at the top (bottom, right-hand side, left-hand side) of the envelope.

5. The words were in the middle of the envelope.

6. He is one of Mr. Beck's friends.
   He is a friend of Mr. Beck's.
   He is a friend of his.
   He is one of my friends. He is a friend of mine.
   He is one of your friends. He's a friend of yours.
   He is one of her friends. He's a friend of hers.
   He is one of our friends. He's a friend of ours.
   He is one of their friends. He's a friend of theirs.

7. The name is not on the envelope.
   It is missing from the envelope.
   The stamp is on the envelope.
   It is not missing from the envelope.
   The letter is not in the envelope.
   It is _____.
   The envelope is not on the table.

(3)

Fill in the missing words:

— man named Nathan Beck lives in Columbus, Ohio. Columbus has — population of over 374,000. One day not long ago, — postman delivered — letter to Mr. Beck. — words "Columbus, Ohio" were written at — bottom of the envelope, and there was — stamp in — upper right-hand corner of — envelope. But Beck's name was not on — letter. — name and street address was missing, too. In place of — name and street address, there was — photograph of Beck on — outside of — envelope.

Beck opened — envelope. Inside, he found — letter from a friend of his in California. — letter said, "I just wanted to see if you really were a big shot in your home town."

Tell the story using these key words as guides:

Nathan Beck	"Columbus, Ohio"	photograph
Columbus, Ohio	bottom	open
population	envelope	envelope
374,000	stamp	letter
postman	upper right	friend
deliver	name	"big shot"
letter	street address	home town

Further activity:

Tell about some letters which you have sent or received recently.

(4)

tice on "has a population of —————" instead of "has population of 374,000" or "has the population 374,000" or something like that. Number 2 gives practice in our system for designating corners. Numbers 3 through 5 give practice with two troublesome prepositions. Control is relaxed still further here, although once a student has grasped the principle in each exercise he probably won't have much trouble.

Missing words: Here control is relaxed with respect to only one grammatical problem—the use of articles. This is a very important problem, however, and requires much drill.

Retelling from key words: This represents a major relaxation of controls, but by now the students should be ready for it.

Further activity: To the student it may seem as though we have now removed all controls; actually we have not, for we are keeping him to a situation in which he can use what he has just finished practicing.

For another sequence of activities in which control is relaxed gradually, see the section on teaching grammar, p. 48.

d) Some suggestions for using pictures. A collection of pictures will stand you in good stead with almost any type of class; it will be especially helpful with beginners. Start saving magazine pictures and have your friends save them for you, too. Here are some ways in which you can use them:

(1) Use them for their decorative value. Learning a new language is a long, hard process at best. Anything you can do to make the room more attractive will help.

(2) Use them to illustrate what you are teaching, whether vocabulary or grammar. We said on p. 24 that

while a student is practicing, he needs to have constantly in mind the *meaning* of what he is practicing. That's hard for him to do if your drill sentences jump from one situation to another:

> The barn is red.
> This street car is green.
> This lake is blue.

Pictures can help.

If you use them to teach vocabulary, you will probably need simple, uncluttered pictures. The object, action, or quality that you want to talk about should stand out clearly. You can use this type of picture also for certain methods of teaching grammar. For example, show pairs of pictures illustrating:

> The banana is yellow, but the car isn't.
> The snow is cold, but the coffee isn't.
> The cow is on a farm, but the lion isn't.

For grammatical structures of other types you may find that you need pictures that tell a story. These pictures are apt to be fairly cluttered with details. If they are, you can't expect your students to take them in at a glance as soon as you show them to the class. Put such a picture on a bulletin board for a while before class so that students can look at it at their leisure.

"Story" pictures present a further problem: the story which is obvious to a native American may be totally hidden from someone who is just learning English. I've seen very few foreign students who could get the full point of a typical *Saturday Evening Post* cover without help. For this reason it is not enough that your picture illustrate your story or other exercise. The story or exercise, in its turn, must help the student interpret the picture.

Here, for example, are three exercises written to accompany the *Saturday Evening Post* cover for September 20, 1952. The picture shows a mother and two boys, about five and eight. They have gotten the older boy's suit out of mothballs so that he can wear it to school. The older boy is wearing the coat, whereas his brother is wearing the trousers.

Elementary level

What are these boys' names?
  Their names are Paul and David Stark. The older one is Paul and the younger one is David.
What is Paul wearing?
  He is wearing a coat and a shirt.
What is David wearing?
  He is wearing a pair of trousers and a shirt.
What is Mrs. Stark wearing?
  She is wearing an apron and a dress.
What kind of shirts are the boys wearing?
  They are wearing sport[1] shirts.
What kind of shoes is Mrs. Stark wearing?
  She is wearing black high-heeled shoes.
What kind of shoe is on the closet floor?
  It's a tennis shoe.
What is that on the closet door?
  It's a garment bag.

---

[1] Notice the recurring stress (accent) pattern in "sport shirt," "tennis shoe," "garment bag," "baseball," and even "baseball bat." This stress pattern is different from the one we have on "closet door," where the second word receives greater stress.

36

What kind of ball is that on the closet floor?
   It's a baseball.
What is that beside the baseball?
   It's a baseball bat.

Intermediate level [2]

American children go to school nine months in every year. They go to school in the fall, the winter, and the spring, but not in the summer. The school year usually begins in September.

It is 8:00 on the morning of the first day of school. Mrs. Stark has put on a good dress and her best shoes because she is going to take her boys to school. She is going to take them to school because this is the opening day of the school year.

Mrs. Stark:	Boys, put your good clothes on. We have to leave the house in twenty minutes.
Paul:	Mother, what shall I wear?
Mrs. Stark:	Put your blue suit on.
Paul:	But my blue suit isn't comfortable, and I haven't worn it since last May. It's too hot. My regular school chothes are much more comfortable!
Mrs. Stark:	Yes, but today is the first day of school, and you ought to look nice. You've grown a lot since May, but I think you can still wear your blue suit.
Paul:	Mother, the trousers fit me, but the coat is too small for me. What shall I do?

[2] This level of grammar is just a little beyond that which is included in the exercise on pp. 108 ff., and is strictly controlled. Notice the context which this picture affords for practicing: (1) "put —— on," "take —— off" (two-word verbs), (2) use of present perfect tense with "since," (3) "too (big) for (me)," (4) "shall" in the sense of "What *shall* we do?" Notice also how the opening paragraphs help the students interpret the picture.

37

Mrs. Stark: Take your suit off. Maybe David can wear it. He's grown a lot since May, too.

David: Mother, the coat fits me, but the trousers are too long for me. Paul's belt is too big for me, too.

Mrs. Stark: Yes, the trousers are too long and the belt is too big. You have grown a lot since May, but you haven't grown enough yet. You will be big enough for Paul's suit next spring, but what shall we do in the meantime? I'm afraid you'll have to wear your regular school clothes.

Paul and David: Oh, boy!

Advanced level
(colloquial American English with few restrictions on grammar or vocabulary)

Everybody has problems. But it seems as if people with growing boys have more problems than anybody. At least, they have *different* problems. Take for example Mrs. Sargent.[3] She has two boys—Billy, who is eight, and Walt, who has just turned six. The boys get along together fine, but they are so active that their mother has a hard time keeping their clothes clean and mended. Mrs. Sargent has taught them, though, that their Sunday clothes are not meant to be played in; the blue suit that she bought for Billy a year and a half ago is still in pretty good shape.

The first Sunday last fall she got out Billy's suit and tried it on him. Billy moved his arms back and forth a little and then said, "Mother, the coat is too tight for me. It's a lot tighter than it was last spring. The sleeves aren't long enough. The pants are all right, though."

[3] Sargent is the name of the artist who painted the cover. His legible signature appears in the lower right-hand corner of the picture.

38

His mother sighed, but she had to agree with him. "Yes," she said, "I'm afraid you've grown since May. You're just too big for this suit. Maybe Walt can wear it."

About this time, her husband came in, so she asked him, "Dick, do you think Walt can wear Billy's blue suit? It's much too good to throw away."

Mr. Sargent, who is an artist, squinted at the suit and squinted at Walt; and then he said, "I'm afraid Walt hasn't grown quite enough yet. But you can try it on him."

She tried the pants on him, but they were much too long. Mrs. Sargent said, "Well, we'll just have to get two new suits. That's all there is to it."

Her husband moaned. "Where are we going to get enough money to pay for them?" was all he could say.

But they did. Can you guess where he got enough money for two new suits?

One point on selecting pictures: pictures may be invaluable in interpreting our foreign culture, but be careful not to use pictures that may offend your students. Pictures may be offensive either because they violate standards of taste that differ from ours, or because they remind the students too vividly of a material standard of living which is far more elaborate than theirs.

I've had good luck in an adult class with a lending library. Each "volume" in the library consisted of a manila folder. Inside each, on the left, was a picture. On the right was a typed sheet with a story or other commentary. The story was about the picture and was written on a very simple level. (See pp. 108 ff. for some hints on learning to write simply for foreign learners.)

e) Routines. On p. 22 we mentioned how important it is to develop your own set of routines and teach them to your class. If you do so, you will save time and annoyance and be able to use your creative energy for the important problems.

Notice, for example, some of the ways in which an instructor may make inefficient use of class time. In the following episode the class is using a drill on verb tenses. The first two sentences in the drill are:

1. We (arrived, have arrived) a few minutes ago.
2. I (am, have been) in the United States since last September. The instructor begins by asking:

	Mr. Jones, will you read the first sentence?	1
Jones:	"We have arrived a few minutes ago."	2
Instructor:	What? . . . Would you say that again?	3
Jones:	"We . . . have arrived . . . a few minutes ago."	4
Instructor:	Now, is that right?	5
Jones:	Er . . . I think so . . . "We arrived"?	6
Instructor:	Yes, that's right! Very good! Now, can you tell me *why* it's right?	7
Jones:	Well, er . . .	8
Instructor:	Can *anybody* tell me why it's right?	9
Smith:	Because it's action completed in the past?	10
Instructor:	*That's* right! Very good, Mr. Smith! All right, Miss Brown, will you take the next one?	11
Brown:	"I have been since last September in the United States."	12
Instructor:	No, that's *almost* right, but can you tell me what you did wrong?	13
Brown:	Oh. "I *am* since last September in the United States"?	14
Instructor:	No. . . . Class?	15
Class:	(unintelligible mumbles)	16
Smith:	"In the United States since last September."	17
Instructor:	Yes, that's right. "In the United States since last September," Miss Brown.	18

Brown:	Oh. "United States since last September."	19
Instructor:	Mr. Green, will you take the next one?	20
Green:	"I am in the United States since last September."	21
Class:	(laughter)	22
Instructor:	Let's stay awake, Mr. Green. It's people like you that keep us from getting all our assigned work done!	23
Green:	Huh?	24
Instructor:	Take Number 3.	25
Green:	Oh.	26
Miss Fox:	Question. Why isn't it "since last September in the United States"?	27
Instructor:	Well, that's hard to explain. You will find it discussed in your book, so we really shouldn't take time for it here. Actually, the meaning of "in the United States" is more closely related to the meaning of the verb than the meaning of "since September" is. That's why it goes next to the verb. The verb "be" has the meaning of "to be located," or "to be in or at a place." Is that clear?	28
Class:	(unintelligible mumbles)	29
Instructor:	Now, Mr. Green, Number 3.	30

Comments on the dialogue:

Line 3: The student still doesn't know whether he's right or wrong, so . . .

Line 4: He repeats (and thereby practices) the wrong response.

Line 5: The student still is not sure, but . . .

Line 6: He guesses the only other alternative.

Line 7: True, "we arrived" is the right alternative, but the purpose of the exercise was to let the student practice using the "simple past" with "ago." The student still has not done this. Ordinarily, the student gets more good out of practicing the "what" of language and less good out of discussing the "why."

Line 10: This is one explanation, but not one that is of much help to students who don't already use this tense right by habit.

Line 11: The phrase "the next one" didn't cause trouble this time, but wait a few lines!

Line 13: Again the instructor keeps the student guessing!

Line 14: This time, therefore, the student repeats the original mistake and adds a new one.

Lines 17-19: The point of the exercise is lost unless the students practice using "since" and "have been" *together*.

Line 21: This wasted motion could have been avoided if the instructor had said "Number 3."

Line 23: Besides annoying the student by scolding, the instructor is also wasting time—helping to keep the class from getting all its assigned work done!

Line 28: The instructor starts off well in trying to deflect the "why" question, but he fails to resist the temptation to speculate about the answer. Unfortunately the comments which he makes here are both time-consuming and confusing.

What we have said here has been largely negative. You yourself must work out the routines that you will use in your classes. We hope that you will be able to avoid some of the common pitfalls represented in the above episode.

2. Teaching Pronunciation

a) Start early. Once a student has been allowed to transplant his native sounds and rhythms into his English, it's very, very hard for him to change. In fact, one set of materials for beginners (Agard, *et al.*, *El Inglés Hablado*) starts out with twelve lessons which do almost nothing except drill pronunciation. Even if you do not go to this extreme, you and your students will want to devote many of your first hours together to patient and painstaking work on pronunciation problems. In the long run, your student will have reason to thank you if you begin by restricting him to a fairly small set of expressions until his pronunciation of them is practically perfect. "Accuracy must precede fluency!"

b) *Start big.* Unless your student's pronunciation is already quite good, you won't be able to correct every error as it comes along. You will have to choose one set of errors and concentrate on them; make it clear to your student that the other errors will have their turn later on.

When you do so, the first errors to work on are those which involve use of pitch, stress, and rhythm. These features of spoken English form a sort of "envelope" into which we fit vowels and consonants. I sometimes start out having students "sing" the envelope of a new expression by using nonsense syllables like "da-DA-da." Then I let them hear the "words" along with the "tune." Once the envelope is right, it is comparatively easy to fit in the vowels and consonants. On the other hand, if a student gets into the habit of concentrating first (or entirely!) on the vowels and consonants, he may never get away from using the envelopes of his own language. And the wrong envelope can keep him from being understood just as surely as the wrong vowel or consonant can!

c) *Be consistent.* Ideally, perhaps, you should stop your student every time he makes an error. In practice, however, this would be exhausting for you and demoralizing for him. You can be *very* strict only for short periods. At other times you will have to confine yourself to pointing out the gross errors. Just be sure that your student is always aware of how strict you are being at the moment. Hold consistently to one standard during pronunciation periods, to another standard at other times.

d) Spread your work. As we've just said, it is almost impossible to be consistently strict for long periods. Your ear and your student's brain soon begin to grow numb. Four ten-minute periods are worth more than sixty solid minutes of pronunciation drill.

e) Should you use phonetic symbols? In many situations, yes; in some situations, no. They can be very useful (see p. 102), particularly in teaching a language like English, which has so many inconsistencies in its writing system.

In some situations a teacher may decide that phonetic symbols are more trouble than they are worth. He must of course be sure that it is not merely his own lack of understanding of the transcription system which brings him to this decision.

Once you have decided to use a phonetic notation in your work, remember to:

(1) *Avoid confusion between transcription and spelling,* since they use many letter symbols in common. You can do this in one of several ways: for example, you might put slant lines (/   /) around transcription; or you can write transcription always to the left of (or to the right of, or above, or below) the regular spelling. You can hold your students responsible for recognizing the symbols but not for writing them. Thus they practice only one writing system.

(2) *Make clear to your student what the transcription*

44

does and does not cover. Many systems cover vowels and consonants only. Others include stress but distinguish only two levels (p. 99).

f) Teach in terms of contrasts. If you listen to a speaker of Spanish (or of many other languages), you will hear him use sounds that resemble our vowel in "sheep" /šiyp/ and others that resemble our vowel in "ship" /šip/. Yet he may speak of going to the United States on a "sheep," and fail to hear any difference between your pronunciation of "sheep" and "ship." This is because the vowel sound of "sheep" occurs between certain sounds in his Spanish words, whereas the sound of "ship" occurs in other positions. The two never contrast; there is no pair of Spanish words corresponding to English "ship"—"sheep," which are kept apart only by this difference in vowel sounds. For this reason you will want to teach, not simply the pronunciation of /iy/, but the contrast between the /iy/ of "sheep" and the /i/ of "ship." The same will be true for most of the other difficult sounds of English.

Not all your difficulties will come from single sounds. As we point out on p. 97, speakers of Spanish or Hindi, for example, are quite accustomed to making sounds like our *s* and *t*, but have great difficulty making "states" sound different from "estates." You will have to be on the watch for troublesome consonant "clusters," such as those in "*st*ate," "*scr*atch," "wi*dth*," "mo*nths*."

Do 95 per cent or more of your drill with words or other short expressions. Work done on isolated sounds or on nonsense syllables is of limited value. Here is an outline procedure which you may find useful:

(1) Let the students try to imitate you ("sheep," "beat," "see," etc.). If necessary,

(2) Explain how the sound is formed (see Part III, p. 90), then

(3) Try direct imitation again.

(4) Do the same with a similar but contrasting sound ("ship," "bit," "sit," etc.).

(5) Now contrast pairs of words containing the two sounds ("sheep"-"ship," "beat"-"bit," etc.). Ask "Did I come here on a ship? On a sheep?" and let the students answer according to what they think they hear. When they can distinguish between these sounds fairly accurately, then

(6) Let the students ask the questions, and you answer according to what you hear.

(7) Finally, have your students practice these sounds in connected speech. Perhaps they can memorize short expressions or conversations that contain these distinctions. For example, the vowels of "sheep" and "ship" occur in:

> How many meals do you eat in the dining hall?
> Two—lunch and dinner.

> How long have you lived here?
> Since September fifteenth.

> It's impossible to fit my feet into these shoes.

g) *A note on pronouncing long sentences.* Pronunciation practice must include not only sounds, sound clusters, and words; it must include whole sentences as well, and some of the sentences should be long. Otherwise, students get no systematic practice in the rhythm and the intonations used with long units.

(1) If the sentence is so long that your student can't say it all at once, start by giving him the *last* phrase in it— not the first one. Then, working backward toward the beginning, build the sentence up phrase by phrase. This pro-

46

cedure has two advantages: many students find it easier, and you yourself are more likely to keep your intonations constant. If you don't keep them constant, you will confuse your student.

(2) Every now and then, give students practice with sets of sentences that are alike in rhythm and intonation:

> You like carrots, don't you?
> He'll be early, won't he?
> She can help us, can't she?

h) Helping students remember intonations. On pp. 100 ff. we have listed the elements out of which we build up the "melodic contours" that we "sing" along with each phrase as we speak English. These elements include four pitch levels and three types of phrase termination, which go together to form a large number of "intonation contours." How is your student to remember which contour he heard with which phrase?

A number of notations exist for just this purpose. We have used one on p. 101. One trouble with most systems of writing intonation is that if they are tolerably complete, they are cumbersome to use on the blackboard and even more awkward when you try to mimeograph them.

One system of intonation writing which I have used takes advantage of two facts: First, a part of our traditional system of sentence punctuation is intended to indicate intonations. Second, although many intonation contours are used in English, only a few are used very frequently.

Before beginning to apply this system of intonation writing, one must go through and mark every word which receives "phrase stress":

This abominable wéather is driving our children crázy.

47

Note that although "abominable," "driving," and "children" all contain more than one syllable, and though one syllable in each has "word stress," these words do not receive phrase stress in *this* sentence.

The further rules are as follows:

(1) All syllables between the last phrase-stressed syllable and a period are on Pitch 1 (low).

(2) All syllables with phrase stress are on Pitch 3 (high).

(3) All other syllables, unless affected by rules 4-8 (below), are on Pitch 2 (mid).

(4) In a "yes"-"no" question (one which does not begin with "who," "what," "how many," "for whom," or some other interrogative), all syllables from the last one with phrase stress to the question mark are high; the last phrase termination (see p. 100) is "rising." "Have your párents come to seé you recently?"

(5) Otherwise, a period or a question mark indicates a "fading" phrase termination.

(6) A comma indicates a "rising" phrase termination (often from Pitch 2).

(7) Phrase terminations which are between syllables with phrase stress, but which have no punctuation, are "sustained" (see p. 100).

(8) One still needs to use extra markings like those shown on p. 101, but *only* when the intonation violates the seven rules given above.

3. *Teaching Grammar*

a) What does it mean to "teach grammar"? When we "teach pronunciation," we teach the sounds of English.

When we "teach vocabulary," we help our students learn English words and their meanings. Grammar-teaching, by contrast, concerns itself with "what goes with what (and when and in what order)." What endings go with what words? Which verb forms go with which time expressions? Which prepositions follow which verbs? In which sentence environments do we use the singular form of a noun and in which environments do we use the plural form? When do we use which article?

When we "teach grammar," then, we help our students see "what goes with what." Even more important, we help them form new habits—habits of putting the right words together in the right way.

b) Which grammatical points should I teach? Teach whatever does not come naturally to your students. For example, a student whose language distinguishes between masculine and feminine third person pronouns, comparable to the English "he"-"she" distinction, will need little or no work on this contrast. Another student, whose native language has only one word corresponding to both "he" and "she," will need a great deal of drill here.

The most effective time to discuss a point of grammar is shortly after your student has found an example of it in his reading or conversational work. Once he has noticed a new usage and wondered about it, you can bring forth other examples and state whatever rules apply to them.

c) What about rules of grammar? Grammatical rules, carefully formulated and properly used, can be extremely valuable. But you've undoubtedly had the experience of trying to help a student use articles, or the present perfect tense, by giving him a rule and then finding that the

49

rule did him no good at all. In fact, it may have deepened his confusion. He may even have come back a day or so later with examples which were perfectly good English, but which contradicted your rule.

A rule of grammar, after all, is merely a general statement of how the speakers of a language use certain parts of that language.[4] Every language has its own grammar: speakers of English do things that would seem quite inconsistent to a speaker of Korean, and vice versa. For this reason, when we formulate a rule, we must first be sure of our facts, then state the facts in such a way that they will be clear even to a person who does not already use English in the manner described by the rule.

How can explanations of grammar be made clearer, less confusing? Here, to reinforce what we said on p. 21, are three partial answers:

(1) Do not claim for your rule a wider applicability than it really has. A rule which purports to describe the use of the definite article, or the simple present tense, or "some" and "any," may actually cover only a portion of the ways in which these forms are used. When in doubt, make a claim that is too narrow rather than one that is too broad.

(2) Wherever possible, avoid stating your rule in terms of meanings. Too often an appeal to "meaning" is an appeal to the already-formed habits of the native speaker of English. When it is, it can be of little help to your students.

(3) Instead of using meaning, try to state your rule in terms of things that can be observed even by the inexperienced speaker of English: we saw on p. 20 that the choice of "some" or "any" in certain of their uses depends on the

---

[4] Or about how someone thinks they *ought* to use them.

50

presence or absence of a negative; with the simple past tense we may use time expressions ending with "ago"; we do not use these expressions with the present perfect tense unless they begin with "since"; "since"-expressions are not used with the simple past.

There are two parts to an effective answer to a question about grammar. One part consists of an adequate "rule" in the sense which we have just discussed. The second part consists of a number of English expressions which illustrate the rule. A poor rule, because it may be confusing, is often worse than no rule at all. For this reason, *if* you are not sure you know the accurate statement of the facts, it is safer to give the illustrations without the rule (see p. 33 for an example).

d) *Some types of grammar drills.*

(1) *A Basic Selection*

(*a*) *Example* (suitable for high school or adult students after several weeks of intensive study):

Renting a Room

A: Good afternoon.
(room)
(for rent)
I've been told you have a room for rent.
B: Yes, I have.
Would you like to see it?
A: (double)
Is it a double room?
B: (single)
No, it's a single.
A: Oh, I'm sorry.
I need a double.

(*b*) *Description:* A "basic selection" is any passage

51

of connected material, usually concerned with a single situation. "Basic exchanges" (i.e., dialogue) are usually easier to practice than are basic selections of other kinds.

Note that, in principle, your student learns basic sentences as a set of indivisible units. It may seem strange that we have included basic selections as a form of grammar drill. The reason is that the student very soon finds that most of the basic sentences he has memorized are partially like others in form and meaning and partially different from them. It is precisely these similarities and differences which provide the basis for grammatical explanations (p. 50) and alteration drills (p. 54). I have learned to speak in only three foreign languages so far; but time and again, in conversation or in writing, I am rescued from a tight grammatical spot only by being able to remember and modify something I memorized long ago.

(c) *Purpose:* Basic selections provide the student with a ready stock of expressions which will be useful in themselves and as patterns for numerous other expressions.

(d) *Procedure:* Before presenting the lesson, pick out the words and phrases which may be new to your student, as we did in (a), above. When you come to a given sentence, let your student repeat these new forms after you. Be sure he understands what they mean; then give him the full sentence that contains them. Follow some such procedure as this:

(i) Teacher says word or expression.

Class repeats in chorus.

Teacher says word or expression again.

Class repeats.

Be sure meaning is clear.

Go through entire lesson in this way.

(ii) Same as (i), with individual repetition.
Teacher points out errors in pronunciation.

(iii) Same as (i), but using full sentences only and one repetition.

(iv) Same as (ii), but using full sentences only.

(v) Teacher says full sentences; students give meaning in native language.

(vi) Teacher gives native language, or part of the sentence in English; students give English.
(If you do not know the native language of your students, you can replace the last two steps by having your students go through the dialogues several times; correct their pronunciation and prompt where necessary in English.)

(vii) Repeat (v), (vi) until students can do (vi) accurately and unhesitatingly.

(e) *Advantages*

(i) Presents life-like material, allows you to introduce idioms as needed.

(ii) May illustrate not only our language but our culture as well (what we talk about, what we say in reply to what, etc.).

(iii) Students realize that "basic exchanges" are immediately useful in any English-speaking community.

(iv) Since basic exchanges develop a single concrete situation, it is easy to get realistic drill by having pairs or groups of students act them out.

(v) Memorized sentences can be used as a basis for analogical formation of new ones.

(f) *Problems*

(i) Students must practice in more than one set of exchanges for each kind of situation.

53

(ii) Direct transition from memorized basic sentences to free conversation is too sharp.

(iii) In choosing or preparing basic sentences, one must be sure to make them life-like and interesting. At the same time, however, one must be careful not to introduce too many new words or grammatical constructions in one sentence.

(2) *Alteration drills*

(a) *Examples*

> (i) I need a double room.
> a single room.
> a bed.
> a towel.
> a face cloth.
> a piece of soap.

(ii) Change the following affirmative sentences to negative sentences:

> e.g., I need a double room.
> I don't need a double room.
>
> 1. I have a room for rent.
> 2. . . .

(b) *Description:* Two types of alteration drills are shown above. In the first type the alteration to be made is suggested by supplying a word or phrase which the student can substitute in the original sentence. This is a simple type of analogical creation.

In the second type the alteration to be made is grammatical. Since the directions are stated in grammatical terms, the exercise needs to begin with an example or two. Note that no vocabulary should be used in an alteration drill except what the student has learned previously. Similarly, grammatical constructions should all be familiar to the student.[5]

(c) *Purpose:* Alteration drills let the student do some carefully controlled analogizing.

(d) *Procedure:* As described under (a), p. 54. Be sure that your students can do the sentences smoothly as well as accurately, and that accuracy extends to intonation and rhythm as well as to sounds and words.

(e) *Advantages*

(i) Gives practice in forming new expressions by analogy.

(ii) Can be improvised to give drill on any point that is causing trouble.

(iii) Lets students practice same "envelope" of rhythm and intonation, while varying the words within it.

(f) *Problems*

(i) Unless you are careful, you will find yourself asking the student to say something which is unidiomatic, or just unlikely to be said, or both. Thus, "My room has two doors" is all right, but "My room has two pictures" sounds strange. And for a sentence that is idiomatic but unlikely to be used in real life, try changing "We are here" to a negative sentence!

(ii) Even if you avoid these pitfalls, alteration drills by themselves tend to become artificial and hence meaningless, if only because they generally entail jumping from one imaginary situation to another. In real life we just don't have occasion to use the same sentence pattern so often in succession.

[5] For a wealth of ideas on the design of such drills, see *Cumulative Pattern Practices,* a volume from the *Intensive Course in English,* published by the English Language Institute of the University of Michigan.

(iii) Insofar as alteration drills are artificial, their influence on the student's free, *genuine* conversation or composition is weak.

(iv) Although it is fairly easy to improvise alteration drills, it is hard to do so successfully on the spur of the moment, particularly if you are in front of a class.

(3) *Fluency Drills*

   (a) *Example*

Pardon me, madam. I've been told that you have a room for rent.

Yes, I have two rooms.

May I see them?

Yes. One is on the first floor and the other is on the second.

Pardon me. I've been told that you have a room for rent.

Yes, I have a room on the second floor.

Is it furnished?

Partly. It has a bed, a table, and two chairs; but there aren't any curtains or pictures in the room.

Pardon me. I've been told that you have a furnished room for rent.

Yes. It's on the third floor. It faces the street.

That sounds nice. How much is the rent?

Ten dollars a week, with linens.

   (b) *Description:* A set of two or more short conversations. Each member of the set develops the same situation in a slightly different way.

   (c) *Purpose:* To help the student get away from the inflexible "basic sentences" and the disjointed alteration drills, and prepare him for eventual free conversation.

(d) *Procedure*

(i) Student A gives the first sentence. B gives the next one, and they continue to the end of the first conversation. There will often be much fumbling and many mistakes the first time through.

(ii) Go through the drill again with different students.

(iii) Go through two or three more times, until students can do the conversation without mistakes and almost without prompting.

(iv) Go on to next conversation in the set.

(v) After all drills in the set have been used as in the first three steps, let the students improvise their own conversations for the same general situation.

(e) *Advantages*

(i) Provide a transition type of drill, bridging the gap between the basic material and free composition or conversation.

(ii) Provide practice in forming new combinations of old materials, as alteration drills do, but in more life-like context and with larger units.

(f) *Problems*

(i) Writer must be sure that he avoids vocabulary or grammatical structures that are unfamiliar to the student.

(ii) For this reason, and because they are longer than alteration drills, fluency drills are harder to prepare.

4. *Teaching Vocabulary*

Much valuable work has been done on English vocabulary and ways of teaching it. Michael West's "New Method" vocabulary of 1,490 words and the "Basic English" vocabulary of 850 words are well known. *English Language*

Teaching contains such articles as one on "A Limited Vocabulary for Scientific and Technical Ideas" (February,
1950). *Language Learning* (July-December, 1950) has
one entitled "On 'I Can't Open the Light, the Open-shut Is
Bad.' " Thorndike and Lorge[6] made a count of millions
of running words in English language publications and
have provided us with a list of words arranged according
to frequency of use.

Although scholars have learned much about vocabulary,
and although you should learn as much as you can about
their findings, remember this: The student who has mastered a large vocabulary is not necessarily the student who
can speak, read, and write the language effectively. In fact,
as Fries has said, we may find real command of a language
—its patterns of sounds and of grammar—*within a very
restricted vocabulary*. First we must establish the basic
phonetic and structural patterns, within whatever restricted
vocabulary is most useful to our students. Then our students
are in a position to go ahead and add extra vocabulary as
fast as they need it, in whatever field of interest they need
it.

Many people believe that it is possible to master vocabulary by memorizing lists of words with their equivalents in
the student's language. Unfortunately that is not true. We
don't even really know the "dictionary meaning" of a word
until we are familiar with the life situations which call it
forth. We certainly do not know its "grammatical meaning" until we know how it behaves with prepositions, articles, auxiliary verbs, and the like. For both these reasons
vocabulary needs to be learned *in context*. (That is why the

[6] See *The Teacher's Word Book of 30,000 Words*.

little glossary following the Basic Selection on p. 32 contains no isolated words.)

I once visited a class in English vocabulary. The teacher had an alphabetical list of English words from the five-hundredth most frequent to the one-thousandth most frequent. As he came to each word, he would "put it into context" by using it in two or three common sentences. Fine as far as he went! How could he have done better?

He could have done what many successful teachers do, grouping together words which are frequently used together in the same conversation: "shore," "ocean," and "island"; or "officer," "meeting," and "report." If he had, the words in each group would have supported each other, one helping the student to understand the meaning of the others. The words might never have been drilled outside of sentences. (I "studied vocabulary" in this way *exclusively* for two of the languages in which I have some conversational fluency, and I find that this method actually helps me remember words that I have half-forgotten.)

Finally, it is sometimes to our advantage to treat a group of words as a single "vocabulary item." This is certainly true of two-word verbs like "stand up," "break up," "cut up," "turn around," "fall down." It may also be true for expressions like "talk politics," "whistle stop," "have a bearing on."

Here is an example of a vocabulary lesson on politics, suitable for rather advanced students.[7] New vocabulary items are italicized.

Everyone likes to *talk politics,* especially in an *election year,* but not everyone realizes the problems facing a *presidential*

[7] The same principle is applied on the elementary level in the "conversation" on p. 36.

candidate. If the candidate wants to win (and of course he does), he has to *stump* the country and make speeches at *whistle stops* as well as in large cities. He has to tell the voters what he will do if he is elected president. Of course, if he wants to appear confident, he tells them what he will do "when" he is elected. Everything that he does or says—as well as everything that he doesn't do or say—*has a bearing on* his *chances for* success. He always *hits out* hard at his opponents. He must *commit himself* on the major issues; yet if he is not careful, he will *alienate* some of his *supporters* and cause a *cleavage* within the ranks of his party.

He must try not to *run afoul* of sectionalism. For example, when he speaks in the South, he must be cautious in talking about *states rights,* the *filibuster,* and the *FEPC*.

If he wants *bosses* to *throw their weight* behind him, he usually has to *make deals* with them. That is, he has to promise them *patronage* and *key positions* for their supporters.

When the last week of the campaign arrives, each candidate makes an *all-out* effort to bring the voters *into his camp*. At the same time, however, he confidently predicts that he will win by a *landslide*.

For another technique which your students can use in learning vocabulary, see p. 68.

5. *Conversation Classes*

Teaching a class in English conversation may mean many things. At one extreme, you may be the entire faculty, as well as the board of trustees and the janitorial staff. At the other extreme, you may be in an established school in which English has been a major subject for many years, and you may be teamed with a teacher who is a native of the country where you are working. No two jobs are alike. For this reason we are unable to give a single neat set of directions for conducting a conversation class. The suggestions that follow are aimed at some of the more common situations.

First of all, let's talk about the materials you will use. If you are in an established school overseas teamed with a local teacher, you probably won't have much choice. Perhaps you will use as a basis for your conversation hours the same materials which he is using for his reading class. True, these materials may or may not be well suited to conversational practice. If they are, so much the better. Or maybe you think they aren't. Two warnings here: First, you may be wrong. Don't judge hastily. Perhaps you can find a way to adapt the materials for your purposes. Second, suitable materials are important, but even more important is morale. If you make a show of your dissatisfaction, staff morale is going to suffer and so is student morale. So if you are in an established school, be sure to co-operate. This doesn't mean that you shouldn't make suggestions after you've been around for a while. But even then you've got to remember to be tactful.

In many situations, though, you *will* have something to say about the materials you are to use. If you do, there are several choices you will have to make. One choice is between sequenced and unsequenced materials. Sequenced materials are those in which vocabulary or grammatical patterns, or both, are introduced at a controlled rate; and each lesson uses only what has previously been learned plus a small amount of new material. Once your students have gotten started in one of these sequences, they have to deal with only a few new problems in each lesson. This is obviously an advantage.

But there are problems connected with sequenced materials, too. The most obvious is that if you are to use them, you should have a fairly stable class—one in which you can keep substantially the same students for, say nine months, three or more hours per week. Otherwise you lose the benefits of the sequencing.

If you are fairly sure of having a stable class, you can choose among several sets of sequenced materials. There are the so-called "Basic English" or "Graded Direct Method" materials,[8] which use a special limited vocabulary and which sequence primarily in terms of the words introduced.

Another extensive set of sequenced materials, sometimes called the "Fries materials" or the "Michigan materials," were produced at the University of Michigan's English Language Institute, by Charles C. Fries and his associates. There are several sets of them, the most fully developed of which is the *Intensive Course in English for Latin Americans*[9] (recently revised under the title *An Intensive Course in English*). The Fries materials concentrate on leading the student to master the structural patterns of the language, and sequencing is primarily in terms of those patterns.

Another set of sequenced materials that you may run across is that being produced under the auspices of the American Council of Learned Societies. This set, like the Fries materials, takes into account the fact that in learning English speakers of French have quite different problems from those which face a speaker of Persian, and such problems of a speaker of Korean or of Indonesian are different still.[10] Yet the underlying analysis of English itself is of

[8] See Richards and Gibson, *Learning Basic English* and *English Through Pictures.*
[9] See also Rojas, *et al.*, *Fries American English Series.*
[10] The Spanish version of these materials has been published commercially as *El Inglés Hablado*, by Agard and staff.

course the same, no matter what the native language of the learner.

As you may have gathered from what I have just said about the Fries and the ACLS materials, they are vast, carefully organized sets of lessons; and it took a great deal of work on the part of many, many people to put them together. The people who did the work were not only numerous; many of them were men and women highly skilled in linguistic analysis and credited with long and successful teaching experience. These facts ought to make us slow to go off by ourselves and try to make up our own lessons whenever the available sequenced materials don't seem to be exactly what we need in a particular situation.

On the other hand, the very mass of these materials, with their careful interweaving of grammatical pattern, vocabulary, intonation drill, and the like, may mean that they are relatively inflexible when it comes to adapting them to situations very much different from those for which they were written. Any textbook writer has to choose one common type of pupil and write in terms of that pupil's interests. One book may be written in terms of the situations encountered by the foreign student living in a university housing unit in which the use of English is required. Another may be slanted toward the displaced person, who is struggling at the same time to hold a job and to improve his English. Now, it's true that either type of student could, from the purely technical linguistic point of view, very well take materials written primarily for the other, master them, and then easily make the changes of vocabulary necessary for his own situation. Technically, that is. But that would require a kind of motivation that is exceedingly rare. You'll find it much, much easier to hold your student's interest if the subject matter in terms of which you introduce these universally used grammatical patterns is close to their experiences and their "felt needs."

If your students' situations are very different from the general situation for which the available sequenced materials were created, or if, as we said, you don't have a fairly stable class, then you may decide it would be wiser to do some improvising on your own. That doesn't mean you should ignore the sequenced materials. To do so would be wasteful. They can still supply easily adaptable ideas for drills, whole sections that can be used, and the grammatical explanations that will help both you and your students to see more clearly what you are doing.

Now let's suppose you do find it necessary to do some adapting or original writing. You can't just walk into a class and start "having conversation." (If you can, your students probably don't need you and would be better off studying agronomy, typing, or New Testament theology.) If you do start right in with no preparation, your students are almost sure to make mistake after mistake, so fast you can't count them; every time they *make* a mistake, they are *practicing* a mistake.

In order to avoid this, you should start out with something that is definitely correct English: a basic selection (pp. 32-33, 51). Hold them pretty close to this at first, and then, by carefully relaxing a series of what we have called "controls," you can lead them to free conversation with many fewer mistakes than you could otherwise.

One way of progressing from closer to looser control is to move from basic selection to alteration drill, and thence to free conversation. Another way is to ask progressively more difficult questions about the basic selection:

a) "Yes"-"no" questions are the easiest, because the student has only to hear the question accurately and choose the appropriate monosyllabic answer. For example, "Do you need a single room?"

b) Next easiest are "or"-questions, because the student can use as his answer a part of what he heard in the question: "Do you need a single room or a double room?"

c) More difficult, in general, are questions beginning with interrogative words like "who," "what," and "why," because the words of the answer are not contained in the question: "What kind of room do you need?"

Let's see what some of these possible basic selections are. In the ACLS materials they are short conversations such as might actually take place on an American college campus. A series of lessons put out by the International Christian University in Tokyo[11] also uses model selections which consist of conversation; these are about a wide variety of topics of general interest. You, too, can make up such conversations, preferably to go with situations in which your students find themselves every day or (for more advanced students) with situations in which they expect to find themselves some day.

Another kind of model is a reading selection. This, for example, is what you may get if you are working as part of a larger program and are teamed with someone else who teaches reading.

Still another kind is the purely oral model: an anecdote or anything else that you tell extemporaneously. I know one very successful teacher who held class in her room once a week. At the beginning of the hour she asked the students to suggest a topic that they would like to hear her talk

[11] McKenzie's *Materials for Standard English Courses.*

on. She then extemporized for five or ten minutes. When she had finished, she went around the room asking questions on what she had said.

When you use basic selections, of course, you have to be sure in some way that the students have a clear idea of what you said, before you begin asking questions on it. The sequenced materials I have mentioned take care of this in one way or another. If you have a colleague who goes over the same selection in reading class, you don't have any worries on this score. And if you can handle the local language fairly well, you can check comprehension easily enough.

6. Reading and Writing

The teaching of reading and writing in a foreign language has been much discussed. It is impossible to present here anything like a comprehensive view of the problems involved or of the many methods which have been developed for dealing with them. We shall limit ourselves to a few brief remarks.

a) Reading

(1) It's a good idea to go over a new assignment with your class before you let them work on it at home. The purpose in doing so is not so much to relieve your students of part of their work as it is to help them expend their effort efficiently. By giving them a bird's-eye view of the assignment, you can keep them from getting lost in details.

You can use the "oral approach" here, too. Perhaps you will have time to read aloud through the entire assignment with your class and let them ask questions about it before they prepare it at home. Or perhaps you will have time for no more than a quick synopsis in English, with comments on a few phrases which you know are likely to cause trouble. Either way, your students are meeting spoken and written English together, and *hearing* precedes reading.

Your synopses or paraphrases will be more effective if at all times you have an accurate idea of which words and which grammatical constructions your students already know and can train yourself to do most of your extemporaneous explanation within these limits. It's a little difficult at first but it's well worthwhile. Practice with the set of exercises given on pp. 108 ff. If you're still not sure your students are with you, you can ask simple (p. 65) questions about what you have just said. You can also help put across the general meaning of many types of material by slightly exaggerating your expression and your gestures to fit what you are reading.

(2) Make clear to your students whether their preparation is to be "intensive" or "extensive." In intensive reading, the student is expected to know the meaning of every word and phrase; in extensive reading he strives for the meaning of the passage as a whole and guesses at the meanings of unfamiliar words unless they prove indispensable to the meaning of the passage. For example, a student reading intensively would look up every word he did not know in the following sentence:

The principal domesticated animals of this region are the cow, horse, goat, sheep, and pig.

Reading extensively, on the other hand, if he already knew "animal," "cow," "horse," and "sheep," he might guess correctly the meaning of "domesticated," assume that "goat" and "pig" refer to other types of domesticated animals, and go on to the next sentence. In this way he would be able to read many more pages per hour than he would if he were reading "intensively."

(3) What about the use of dictionaries and glossaries? Here are a few suggestions:

(a) As soon as possible the student should begin using an English-English dictionary. For *foreign* learners of English, four of the most useful are *The Thorndike-Barnhart Comprehensive Desk Dictionary, The Thorndike Century Senior Dictionary,* West and Endicott's *New Method English Dictionary,* and *The Advanced Learner's Dictionary of Current English,* edited by Hornby, Gatenby, and Wakefield.

(b) Discourage your students from writing the equivalents in their language above the English words that they've had to look up. If they do, you may be sure that every time they go over the passage their eyes will skip up to the native words. They will never see the English words again.

(c) If your students make out word lists for study, have them put each word on a separate card or slip of paper. The cards can be shuffled so that the student meets the words in various orders. As some words are learned faster than others, the cards bearing those words may be set aside to make room for others. Packets of cards are easy to carry around so that they may be studied in spare moments. It is more valuable to have many brief periods of study than it is to spend the same amount of time in one continuous period.

(d) No matter how your student does it, however, making out word lists is a tedious job. Here's an alternative: The first time your student has to look up a particular word, have him put beside it a dot in the margin of his glossary or dictionary. Perhaps he will remember the word ever after. If he does, there was no need to make a card for it. If he doesn't, he will have to look it up again and place a second dot in the margin of the glossary. By the time a third dot appears, he knows that for some reason this word is giving him trouble; it will be worth his while to make a card for it.

(4) We've talked about preparing the reading assignment both in the preceding class and between classes. Here are a few suggestions relating to recitation:

For one thing, try not to have the students just translate sentence after sentence. Somewhere along the line, be sure they can read their sentences aloud so that they sound meaningful. This means pausing in the right places and using acceptable intonation and stress. And this is not merely for the benefit of the oral English, either. Putting words together in the groups in which they belong is just as necessary for efficient reading as it is for efficient hearing and speaking. If your students are so advanced that they can do this without hearing you do it first, well and good. But if they can't, it will be worth your while, before you have the sentences translated, to read them aloud and have individuals or the class repeat after you.

It is by no means necessary to assume that your students will *translate* at all. In fact, unless and until you can understand their language rather well, you have no way of being sure their translation is accurate.

Even if you do understand your students' language, translation is not necessary. After all, you and I read English without having to translate it into some other language to be sure we have understood it. What you are aiming at in reading class is primarily to train your students to look at a page of English and get from it the same information they

69

might get from a corresponding page in their native language. For this purpose you may actually find that use of the native language is more trouble than it's worth—that it is training them to *decipher* English rather than to read it.

In most situations you can find ways of doing without the students' native language. If you want to check comprehension, what better way than by asking questions—more or less simple questions—in English? Take for example a sentence from Thoreau's *Walden,* a comparatively difficult book for foreign students:

> Shall we forever resign the pleasure of construction to the carpenter?

It would be fairly simple to be sure your students understood the meaning of "carpenter." Ask some question like "What does a carpenter do?" or an even simpler question like "Does a carpenter build houses?" and so forth. Then, to get at the meaning of the sentence as a whole, "Does Thoreau think it is fun to build things?" "What does Thoreau think? Should the carpenter do all the building? Should people who are not carpenters build things, too? Why should they build things?"

That's just one example, taken from a fairly difficult piece of prose.

b) Writing. The same principles apply to writing class that apply to conversational work. That is, the student needs a model to follow more or less closely and he needs to be restrained from trying too much too soon.

(1) One kind of model is a reading selection. For very close control you might assign simple alteration drills (p. 54) based on sentences or parts of sentences from the reading selection. Looser control would result from having

the students retell the selection from memory. Finally, have them write original compositions on a related topic. For example, if the reading selection was about the chores for which children are responsible in American homes,[12] have your students write about the responsibilities of children in the homes where they themselves grew up.

(2) Another kind of model is an oral selection. Anecdotes are particularly suitable for this purpose because they are sufficiently short and well enough unified to stay in the student's mind until he can write them down. You will want to simplify the anecdote sufficiently so that little or none of the vocabulary or grammar is over your students' heads. Then you will need to tell the anecdote several times and perhaps allow your students to ask questions about it in English before they try to write it in their own words. You will probably find it best to ask your students not to try to make notes while they are listening to you. (For an example, see p. 32.)

(3) If your students still make a large number of mistakes, you might try requiring them to limit the length of their sentences. A two-clause limit is a practicable one which still allows for plenty of variety in sentence structure.

(4) Finally, what is your student to do about his errors, once you have pointed them out to him? If he has made many in a single paper, you may want to suggest that he concentrate his attention on only a few of them. In any event, be sure that he practices the correct forms, not the errors. You can help him by giving him three or four sentences which are structurally parallel to the corrected sentence and having him practice these.

[12] See Kitchin and Allen, *Reader's Digest Readings in English as a Second Language,* for such a selection.

7. *Some Notes on Conversation, Reading, and Writing*

In the last few pages we have treated conversation, reading, and writing as though they were separate activities. Actually, of course, there are great advantages in talking over in class what you have just read about or what you are going to ask your students to write about.

a) Verbalizing Experience. One of the most meaningful and interesting assignments is one which puts into words the experiences of the students themselves. This verbalization of experience will work in reading, writing, or conversation classes, with beginning, intermediate, or advanced students. It ranges from holding up a pencil and saying, "A pencil," all the way to discussing a recent trip to Mount Fuji.

Or you may draw on specific experiences which are *not* shared by all members of the class. One of the most successful teachers I know does this with fairly advanced adult students: she places a loaf of bread (or some other familiar object) in the center of the room and asks each person to tell about some memory relating to bread. Besides providing good practice with English, this technique develops in each student a feeling of importance and participation in the group.

This sharing of diverse memories is constructive in another way, also, particularly in groups where nationalities are mixed: it dramatizes for each member of the group the fact that his own cultural heritage is irreplaceable and respected and can make its unique contribution to the life of his new group or nation.

One successful teacher with whom I am acquainted achieved excellent results by asking her high school girls to verbalize experiences that they had never had! One wrote

72

on "I am a pair of chopsticks," another on her experiences as a tree that stood near their campus, and so on!

b) *Dictation.* Dictation can form a very useful part of your teaching routine. Actually, the term "dictation" is used for a variety of activities.

Before discussing some of the ways in which you can use dictation, here are two recommendations that we can make without qualification: First, develop one or two dictation procedures that fit your needs, and stay with them. Second, when you are dictating connected material, dictate sentence by sentence or phrase by phrase, with natural rhythm and intonation—never word by word.

In developing your own dictation procedures, you must decide how you want to answer these questions:

(1) *Are you testing spelling?* Many successful teachers test spelling apart from their dictation exercises; when they give dictation, they write on the blackboard all the less common words that they use. In this way they are *teaching* spelling, not *testing* it.

(2) *How are you going to dictate?* By sentences or by phrases? How often will you repeat each unit?

(3) *What are you going to dictate?* The most obvious material consists of ordinary prose. Many teachers, however, use dictation for systematic ear training by giving pairs or sets of sentences that sound almost alike:

> "What has he done?" "What has she done?"
> "The boy is here." "The boys are here."
> "I need a new mop." "I need a new map."

(4) *When are you going to dictate?* Many teachers wait until *after* they have covered a passage in some other way before they use it for dictation. Then they use the

73

original passage itself or make small changes in the passage.

(5) *What happens after the dictation?* Will each student rewrite correctly the whole sentences in which he has made mistakes?

8. *What About Audio-Visual Aids?*

What is an audio-visual aid? If it is anything audible or visible which helps your student learn the language more quickly or more accurately, then you yourself ought to be one. Your textbook is a visual aid, and so is your blackboard. We have discussed on pp. 34 ff. some of the ways in which magazine pictures can serve as visual aids. In this section we will comment briefly on five of the less commonly used types of audio-visual aids. They are the flannelgraph, the opaque projector, the film strip, the tape recorder, and the movie. For more detailed discussions of these and many other audio-visual aids, see Dale's *Audio-Visual Methods in Teaching.*

a) The flannelgraph. Have you ever noticed that two pieces of flannel will stick to each other if you press them together, even when you hold them in a vertical position? The flannelgraph, which takes advantage of this principle, is a visual aid that is both inexpensive and surprisingly flexible. Cover a large board with flannel and draw on it an outdoor scene, a street, or some other large picture. Then on smaller pieces of flannel draw or paste smaller pictures—of people, animals, or movable objects. You can now make these smaller pictures take appropriate places in the larger scene and move them around to illustrate various sentences or to follow the progress of a story.

b) The opaque projector. This device allows you to take any book or paper and project it onto a wall or screen.

There are great advantages in being able to do so when you are trying to use small pictures with large classes. Or perhaps you will want to project a student's paper on the screen and discuss with the class some of the ways in which the paper could be improved.

In order to spare embarrassment to individual students and at the same time make the lesson of first-hand interest to more than a single student at a time, you might try this: Type out a paragraph which contains mistakes gleaned from several papers. If your class is not too large, you may be able to include at least one mistake from everyone's paper. Let the students pick the mistakes out and then correct them. Every time a mistake is found or corrected, you can remove the paper from the projector, mark it, and put it back in.

There are several problems connected with the use of opaque projectors. For one thing, they require electricity— a lot of it. Some of them put out a good deal of heat and may contain noisy fans in their cooling systems. They are bulky and may be too expensive for your budget. Finally, if you use one too long at a time in a darkened room, with the heat from its lamp and the hum of its fan, you may put your students to sleep! Most of these objectionable features, however, have been eliminated from the newer models.

c) *The film strip.* Like the opaque projector, the film strip projector lets you use small pictures with large classes. Unlike the opaque projector, you can project only what you can find—or put—on a specially prepared piece of film. Having your own film strips manufactured is not a hopelessly expensive undertaking.

Many fine film strips are already in existence, however.

A few of them are specially designed for classes in the English language. Using one of these film strips, you can quickly and easily present a series of clearly visible pictures, instead of having to fumble around for the right magazine cover, concrete object, or whatever you wish to show to your class.

Countless other film strips, in color as well as in black and white, were prepared for other purposes but can be extremely interesting to intermediate or advanced classes. *Life* magazine, for example, has several series—some on art, some on the history of western culture, others on different countries of the world, and so on. The *New York Times* publishes a film strip on current events every month from October through May. You can also get films and film strips from state universities and state departments of education, as well as from a number of commercial sources. Fitting the vocabulary and the grammar to the ability and the needs of your class, you can write your own commentary on such film strips. After you have shown such a film strip one or more times, you can show it again and ask questions on it or have the students comment on the pictures or let them ask questions for further information.

One problem with film strips: you have to use them in such a way that your students participate somehow every few seconds; otherwise they may fall into a passive role in the class and from there to inattention.

d) The tape recorder. A tape recorder, like a phonograph, makes it possible for your students to listen to English spoken by a native speaker of the language, even when you are busy doing something else. Unlike the phonograph, the tape recorder lets you record exactly the stories, the sentences, or the words that you want your students to hear. It also lets you erase what you no longer need or what you don't like, and record something else in its place. The tape recorder can be invaluable in multiplying your students' listening hours. The tape recorder offers one other advantage: your students can listen to themselves as well as to a recorded native speaker. Hearing onself on a machine is a wonderful way to become vividly aware of one's own shortcomings. That is particularly true if the native speaker's voice is recorded together with one's own.

There are two ways to get the two voices on the tape together. One, of course, is for the native and the student to record together. The other is through use of a "binaural" recorder. The binaural recorder uses two sound tracks instead of one. The native can put his voice on one track while the student uses the other. When the tape is in use, only the student's track is erased and re-recorded, whereas the master track remains.

The most conspicuous problem with tape recorders, aside from initial expense and occasional difficulties in maintenance, is one of time. It takes time to record, time to rewind, and time to play back. Every time you want to play back, you have to spend a certain amount of time in rewinding and finding your place. You need to plan your procedures carefully in order to keep this lost time to a minimum. As a matter of fact, students can gain many of the benefits of listening to themselves just by using the echo from a corner in the wall or from an opened textbook held to the side of the face.

e) Motion pictures. With the exception of one or two movies made especially for beginning students of English, movies are most suitable for high intermediate or advanced students. Perhaps you will have the facilities and the budget so that you can rent movies and show them in your class-room. If you haven't you can take advantage of whatever English-language movies your students have seen at com-mercial theaters as a basis for discussion of American (or English) life and language. We need hardly caution you that many movies require a good bit of interpretation in order to keep the class from getting a distorted picture of life in the English-speaking world.

There is also on the market a combination magnetic recorder and 16 mm. movie projector. Movie film can be specially "banded" with a magnetic recording track for use with this machine. You can then record your own sound track just as you would make a tape recording, and can use your recording instead of, or along with, the original sound track.

9. *Other Features of Your Teaching Situation*

a) *How old are your students?*

(1) *Children.* Children, more than anyone else, need lessons that don't require them to work in terms of long-range goals. That is, the lessons must be fun in themselves, and they must be close to the children's own experience and interests. Just naming books, pencils, blackboards, and the like will soon get tiresome; so will exercises which drill verbs, etc. You can draw your lesson activities from the things that your students all know about: greetings, family, foods, pets, school. Try to tie your lessons in with the things that the pupils have been learning in classes con-ducted in their own language. In any case, start them out with simple sentences that correspond to things they already say every day, in or out of school.

Remember that the younger the child, the shorter the

attention span. In a class of very young children, about all you can do is play with them in English. Twenty minutes a day may be enough. Even within such a short class period you will probably need to have a variety of activities so that the pupils won't get restless. Wherever possible give them a chance to be active, to move about, to feel that they are "doing something," instead of "just studying."

In place of drills, for instance, you might use games or songs, or let the pupils set out simple dialogues. Try adapting games like "Simon Says" or letting the children play store with empty cans and play money. As for songs and jingles, the only precaution is that they must be in simple, modern, speakable English. "Are You Sleeping?" and "Billy Boy" are fairly good; "Old Folks at Home" or "Clementine" wouldn't be so suitable for this purpose.

Finally, don't push children too hard. The most important aim of the earliest lessons will be to give the pupils a happy experience with the new language. Some schools don't ask pupils to read, write, or even do much individual oral recitation for the first two years.[13]

(2) *Adolescents*. First, a couple of "don'ts" about adolescents. *Don't* assume that they will be charmed by the same kind of stories and games that delight children in the same culture. And *don't* expect them to put up with the dullery that adults (in some cultures, at least) have been trained to endure.

One big difference between adolescents and small children is that your adolescent students will almost surely be

[13] For detailed ideas see Rojas, *et al., Teacher's Guides* for the first volumes of *Fries American English Series;* Hansen, G. F., *A Guide for the Teaching of French in the Elementary Schools;* and the publications put out by such cities as El Paso and San Diego for teaching Spanish to children.

able to read and write. But you can still use an oral approach (see p. 23), whether you are teaching a conversation class or a class in reading and composition.

For reading matter try fiction. But don't limit yourself to fiction. Find out what your pupils are already curious about. Then if you can, give them simplified readings in science, geography, or the like. Simplified readings, by the way, are hard to find and harder to write. What seems perfectly simple to you may turn out to be quite difficult. The same may be true even of reading materials that are advertised as "simplified." Some good simplified reading materials are West's *New Method Readers,* Kitchin and Allen's *Reader's Digest Readings in English as a Second Language,* and Allen's *People in Livingston.*

Young people at this age are capable of high enthusiasm and almost unlimited interests. Also, they are likely to be able to put in more time than adults (who are too busy) or young children (who lack the attention span). Some successful teachers I have known have taken advantage of these characteristics to guide their pupils in all sorts of creative projects. Examine the situation in which you find yourself and see what you and your students can come up with. See *Teacher's Guides* to the later volumes of the *Fries American English Series.*

(3) *Adults.* Have you ever heard "Life with Luigi"? Remember the night-school teacher, Miss Spaulding? Well, *don't* follow her example. She treats her adult students like grown-up children, and that's one thing you must not do.

Do remember that your adult has lived through much more than children have—more than you have, perhaps. He has a good understanding of the world about him, except that it's all in a language other than English. Draw on this background. In reading or in conversation choose topics with which he is already thoroughly familiar. Later, after he has developed some fluency, he can go on to topics which are new to him.

Do remember that adults, even more than children, will "take it hard" if you scold them, so don't. They are even likely to feel humiliated by routine corrections. This poses a serious problem, especially in certain countries. How can you meet this problem? How can you make corrections without making enemies at the same time? As we said on p. 22, you will discover an answer only as you yourself become a member of the local culture and find out how your people do things.

The same is true when you select subject matter. In some cultures adults are happy to practice little stories which would also be suitable for children. In others you have to stick at all times to subject matter which is considered intellectually respectable. There are many books and courses prepared for adults. See Lado's and Cochran's bibliographies for suggestions.

b) How much English do your students already know?

(1) *Beginners.* I've seen quite a few inexperienced teachers quail at the thought of having to teach a group of absolute beginners. When you get right down to it, though, it's not so hard. In some ways it's actually *easier* than working with more advanced students, for the advanced classes are seldom very uniform.

This is your students' first, best, and perhaps last chance to learn an accurate pronunciation. Help them on it all you can. Bear down hard on intonation and rhythm as well as on the contrasts among the vowels and consonants.

Even in a lesson that looks perfectly simple to you, the

number of new things to trouble a beginner is surprising. Not only new sounds, but new sound-clusters; not only new words, but old words in new uses. Maybe an old word will come along with a new meaning. Or maybe two old words will be combined in a way to which your students aren't accustomed. What is important is this: you must be aware of these problems as they arise, and lend the student a hand. The series of exercises on pp. 108 ff. are designed to help you develop this kind of awareness.

(2) *Intermediates.* Other things being equal, this is the level that I personally think is hardest to teach. For one thing, the label "intermediate" is applied to such a wide variety of students. For another, your intermediate is no beginner—he already knows a great deal and wants you to recognize that fact. Usually what one remembers, another never learned. This makes it complicated when you try to decide what to drill on.

On the other hand, the intermediate is not advanced: he is not yet to the place where he can go right into anything, no matter how hard, and derive benefit from it. You still have to select his assigned reading and control his other assignments carefully. No two ways about it, this requires judgment, skill, experience. But here are two rules of thumb which you might try in the meantime:

(*a*) Material is too hard if the students stumble badly more than once in a sentence.

(*b*) When the students write, make them keep their sentences short. Two clauses are plenty.

(3) *Advanced.* In advanced classes students differ widely in what they know and what they want to know, in what they have done and in what they want to do. Take advantage of this diversity. Each might have his own read-

82

ing assignments, his own topics for oral or written composition. His reading and writing will mean more to him if he is telling something to the whole class instead of just to the teacher.

Here are a few things you can do in class:

(a) Discuss the problems of writing a formal report: footnotes, quotations, preparing the bibliography, use of library facilities, etc. These are mechanical details, but they are important and they differ from country to country.

(b) Drill on problems of pronunciation and grammar that are shared by most of the members of the class.

(c) Let them read plays, poems, or other literature. This is good not only for their language; it helps them understand our culture as well. One caution, though: don't start on Shakespeare! Choose things that use English as it is spoken today. For example, *Our Town*, by Thornton Wilder.

(d) Let them listen—to records, to radio broadcasts, etc. You may want to read something aloud yourself and then let them rewrite it in their own words. Listening practice is especially in order if your students expect to listen to lectures in English someday.

(e) Let the students talk to their classmates on topics in which they are specially prepared.

(f) Let them organize debates or panel discussions.

In the last two of these activities, remember that even advanced students lack the sureness in English that native college freshmen possess. They will need plenty of models to follow, from reading or from other sources.

c) *How often does your class meet?*

(1) *One to two hours per week.* You have a problem. With a class that meets so infrequently, you have to be sure that every session is self-contained, except for reviews.

(2) *Three to six hours per week.* If you have this many hours, you can count on some carry-over from one hour to the next. But it is a good idea to make each week's work a natural unit of some kind. It helps you and the students establish a rhythm, and rhythm helps you get more done with less effort.

(3) *Six or more hours per week.* You have enough class hours to help your students accomplish a lot. In a class that is together this many hours a week, you can make good use of whatever you know about group dynamics.

d) *What is the size of your class?*

(1) *One to five students.* This amounts to private or semi-private tutoring.

Remember that this size class is more tiring for individual students than is a larger group. But in a small group you will find plenty of opportunities for momentary relaxation and good humor. Again, knowledge of group dynamics will stand you in good stead.

(2) *Five to twenty students.* Most classes are of this size. This is still small enough so that you can get to know your students by name very early and can remember who has which problems. It will be worth your while to do so, too.

(3) *Twenty to eighty students.* If your class is this large, there are several points to be especially careful of.

(a) Class sessions must be very clearly organized. The main parts must stand out, and there should not be too many details.

(b) You must speak more slowly and distinctly than in a smaller group. Pause frequently unless you are sure everyone is right with you.

Remember that while language-teaching usually combines comprehension practice (reading and hearing) with production practice (writing and speaking), it is not necessary to do so. If your class is very large—say fifty to sixty—perhaps you should concentrate most of your effort on getting your students to *understand* English.

If you want to give the students a chance to speak frequently, see what you can do with choral repetitions.

e) *Is attendance voluntary?*

(1) *Yes.* If you want them to keep coming back, be sure that they get a definite feeling of accomplishment *every hour.* One way to do this is to give a short quiz at the end of almost every hour. Try to make it a quiz that covers what you have taken up in class, yet one that almost all the students can do perfectly. (If you can't devise such a quiz, it probably means there is something wrong with your teaching. Perhaps you have been going too fast.)

(2) *No.* Just remember that your teaching will be more effective, and more fun for you and your students, if you don't take advantage of the fact that they are a captive audience.

f) *Will your students have time for homework?*

(1) *Yes.* Two things to remember about homework:

(a) It should be on work already covered, not new work. (An exception may be advanced reading classes.)

(b) Homework exercises should be drills, but not *puzzles*. Never give exercises in which you know your people will make many mistakes.

(2) *No.* If your people don't have time for homework, they still need drill. This means you must develop some regular series of classroom activities that will provide for practice of old material as well as discussion of new.

g) *Are you working in an established school?*

(1) *Yes.* Don't let anything you have read here or elsewhere keep you from co-operating in the established program.

The most rigidly organized program leaves some leeway for initiative. If you feel the program could be improved, develop your ideas within the allowed margin. Perhaps you will find that your ideas weren't so good after all. Or perhaps you really did have a good idea. If you did, your teaching will improve so that people will begin to ask what you are doing in your classes.

(2) *No.* Two rules:

(a) Don't follow anything slavishly. Experiment! Experiment!

(b) Don't experiment too often. Give your students time to get used to one routine before switching to another.

PART III

Some Useful Information About the English Language

1. *About the Sounds of English*

Mastering the sound system of English means learning to hear and to make sounds in the same way that a native speaker of English does; in particular, this means that your students must come to hear and use a whole new set of sound distinctions, or contrasts. Words that to us sound like "chin" and "shin" may in another language be nothing more than slightly different pronunciations of exactly the same thing; speakers of such a language will have learned to ignore the very sound distinction which enables us to tell whether a person has bumped his "shin" or his "chin."

Specifically, anyone learning English must master at least the contrasts among the vowel and consonant sounds in the key words listed on pp. 88-90. Opposite each key word you will find the ways in which a common pronunciation of that word may be transcribed in three of the many systems of notation now in use.

Each system of notation tries to do exactly the same thing as the others; each tries to represent the realities of spoken English completely and clearly. Systems of notation differ among themselves in three ways:

a) They differ in the letter-shapes which they employ. For the most part, you can take words transcribed in one system and convert them mechanically to another system. All you have to do is substitute symbols from one of the vertical columns (pp. 88-90) for the symbols which appear opposite them in another column.

b) Occasionally, however, one system will provide for a distinction of sound that is ignored by the other systems.

c) Two systems may disagree as to the status which they assign to a sound difference which both admit exists. One system will consider that two different pronunciations of the same word are equivalent, one pronunciation being used in certain dialects, the second in others. Another system of transcription may assign different symbols to those same two pronunciations. The reasoning which underlies such disagreements is extremely interesting but is beyond the scope of our handbook. For an illuminating discussion of this problem see Gleason's *Introduction to Descriptive Linguistics,* Ch. 16.

Vowels

Key Words	Transcription 1[1]	Transcription 2[1]	Transcription 3[1]
b**ea**t, s**ee**	biyt, siy	bit, si	bēt, sē̆
b**i**t, **i**n	bit, in	bɪt, ɪn	bit, in
b**ai**t, r**a**ce	beyt, reys	bet, res	bāt, rās
b**e**t	bet	bɛt	bet
b**a**t	bæt	bæt	bat
kn**o**b, c**o**t	nab, kat	nɑb, kɑt	näb, kät
c**au**ght[2]	kɔht	kɔt	kôt
b**oa**t	bowt	bot	bōt

[1] Transcription 1 is based on Trager and Smith's *Outline of English Structure.* It is gaining acceptance in many places. Transcription 2 is typical of what you will find in many books all over the world. It is taken from Kenyon and Knott's *Pronouncing Dictionary of American English.* Transcription 3 is from *Reader's Digest Readings in English as a Second Language.*

[2] Some speakers of English have no contrast between the vowels of

Vowels

Key Words	Transcription 1[1]	Transcription 2[1]	Transcription 3[1]
f<u>oo</u>t	fut	fʊt	fůt
b<u>oo</u>t	buwt	but	bŭt
b<u>u</u>t[3]	bət	bʌt	but
j<u>u</u>st	jəst	dʒʌst	just
b<u>uy</u>, t<u>ie</u>	bay, tay	baɪ, taɪ	bī, tī
b<u>oy</u>	boy	bɔɪ	boi
ab<u>ou</u>t	əbawt	əbaʊt	əbout

Consonants

	Transcription 1[4]	Transcription 2[4]	Transcription 3[4]
<u>p</u>eak, s<u>p</u>eak	p		
<u>t</u>ie, s<u>t</u>y	t		
<u>c</u>ow, s<u>ch</u>ool	k		
<u>b</u>ite	b		
<u>d</u>o	d		
<u>g</u>o	g		
<u>ch</u>ew	č	tʃ	ch
ju<u>dg</u>e	ǰ	dʒ	j
<u>f</u>ew	f		
<u>th</u>in	θ		th
<u>s</u>o	s		
<u>sh</u>oe	š	ʃ	sh
<u>v</u>iew	v		
<u>th</u>en	ð		ꟻH
<u>z</u>oo	z		
mea<u>s</u>ure	ž	ʒ	zh
<u>l</u>ight	l		
<u>r</u>ight	r		
<u>m</u>ight	m		

"cot" and "caught." If you pronounce these words alike, don't worry about trying to make your students distinguish them.

[3] Many speakers of English use the vowel of "but" in "He's a *just* man," but a different vowel (/ɨ/) in "I've *just* arrived." Note that /ɨ/

Consonants

	Transcription 1[4]	Transcription 2[4]	Transcription 3[4]
<u>n</u>ight	n		
so<u>ng</u>	ŋ		ng
<u>h</u>igh	h		
<u>w</u>e	w		
<u>y</u>ou	y	j	y

These, then, are the vowel and consonant contrasts that your students must learn. Some will "come naturally" to them; others will seem almost impossible.

In the section on teaching pronunciation (pp. 42-48) we gave some suggestions for helping your students work their way over the rough spots with a minimum of frustration. At that time we said that you need to be able to explain how the hard sounds are formed. That is, you must be able to explain what to do with the tongue, the lips, the voice, etc., in order to get closer to the English sound.

Unfortunately your native skill in producing these sounds yourself does not endow you with the ability to explain them. You must first become conscious of many of your own speech habits. The summary given here is only a crude sketch; you can find English phonetics presented much more adequately in several books: for example, Prator's *Manual of English Pronunciation for Adult Foreign Students,* or Thomas' *Introduction to the Phonetics of American English.* Remember though: no amount of reading *about* English sounds can take the place of a few hours of sitting before a mirror and watching your tongue and lips as you experiment with all the sounds you know.

---

is also different from the vowels in "gist" (/jist/) and "jest" (/jest/).

[4] Transcriptions 2 and 3 agree with 1 except where separate entries are made under them.

WARNING: In reading the next few pages for the first time, you will need to equip yourself with a mirror small enough to be held in one hand, and then sit by a window.

Let's talk first about the vowels. The variations which we perceive among vowels of different qualities are produced in a number of ways. Different degrees of lip-rounding, or of tongue tenseness, or of duration in time, play their parts. Most conspicuous, and perhaps most important, is the factor of tongue position.

Try the following experiment. Holding the mirror so that you can watch your tongue, open your mouth as wide as possible. Now, *keeping your mouth wide open,* try to produce the vowel /i/[5] as in "bit" and then the vowel /u/ as in "foot." As you do so, you should see your tongue move from front to back.

Close your mouth now in order to rest your jaw. Open it again. This time try /i/, and /æ/ as in "bat." Your tongue will go from a high position to a low one. Finally, try going from /æ/ to /a/ as in "father." Again your tongue will move from front to back.

In fact, the "simple vowels" as represented in Transcription 1 may be arranged in tabular form according to tongue position. Some writers[6] prefer to present them in terms of a quadrilateral, as in the following chart.

This is where phoneticians get such terms as "high

[5] Any of the three systems of transcription shown on pp. 88-90 could be used in our discussion. The symbols employed here are from Transcription 1.

[6] This arrangement is used, for example, by Gleason and by Trager and Smith (see bibliography), as well as by John Kenyon and Daniel Jones.

front," "low back," "mid-central," which you will find in their discussions of vowels.

	Front	Central	Back
High	/i/ bit	/ɨ/ just	/u/ put
Mid	/e/ bet	/ə/ but	/o/ home (certain dialects only)
Low	/æ/ bat	/a/ father	/ɔ/ wash (certain dialects only)

For a different arrangement, in triangular form, see p. 93.

But we have not yet exhausted the subject of vowels. As a matter of fact, two of the simple vowels in the above table, /o/ and /ɔ/, are comparatively rare in most people's speech. On the other hand, we still have not discussed such common sounds as the vowels of "beat," "boot," or "boat." Yet the difference between "beat" /biyt/ and "bit" /bit/ is a very important one in English, and one which is hard for speakers of many, many languages.

There are several physical differences between these two sounds. For most speakers /iy/ (the vowel of "beat") is a little longer, with the tongue tenser, higher, and farther forward in the mouth. Perhaps most important of all, in producing this vowel the tongue actually glides toward a higher position farther toward the front of the mouth.

The difference between "bet" /bet/ and "bait" /beyt/ is quite analogous to the difference between "bit" and "beat." You will notice that it is symbolized in the same way in Transcription 1—by the letter /y/. The /ay/ sound occurs in most people's pronunciation of "bite." The word "boy" contains /ɔy/ or /oy/.

A comparable difference exists between "could" and

"cooed"; and there is another between /o/, and /ow/ as in "boat." But with these sounds the glide symbolized by /w/ is toward a tongue position which is higher and farther back, together with a continuous increase in lip rounding. The word "about," for most people, contains /aw/.

A third glide is toward a "mid-central" tongue position. That is to say, it is a glide toward (not necessarily *to*) the position for the vowel of "but." This glide is symbolized in Transcription 1 by /h/; Gleason, whose transcription is otherwise identical with Transcription 1, uses /H/. We hear it in many pronunciations of "bought." We also are very likely to hear it before final /r/: "here" /hihr/, "there" /ðehr/, "four" /fohr/. These last three words, in dialects which do not pronounce /r/ in final position, may be /hih/, /ðeh/, and /foh/, respectively.

Many phoneticians prefer to list together the simple vowels and the "vowels-plus-glides" that are most common in American or in British English. They frequently arrange them in a triangle according to tongue and jaw position:

/iy/ beat		/uw/ boot
/i/ bit	/ɨ/ just	/u/ foot
/ey/ bait	/ə/ but	/ow/ boat
/e/ bet		/ɔh/ bought
/æ/ bat	/ɔ/ wash (Southern	
/a/ father		British, and some other forms of English)

Having touched on some of the most important vowels, let's go on to look at the consonants. Like the simple vowels on p. 92, most of the consonants may be arranged in a fairly neat diagram.

First watch yourself make the beginning sounds of "pie," "buy," "my." You will notice that for all these sounds your lips touch each other. In technical language /p, b, m/ are all "bilabials." (We include a few of these technical terms here because you are likely to need them if you read discussions of phonetics.)

Then watch your tongue as you form the first sounds of "tie," "die," "nigh." Your tongue tip (apex) touches your

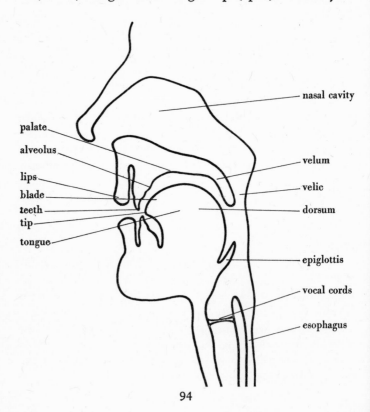

94

gum ridge (alveolus). These sounds are "apico-alveolar," sometimes called simply "alveolars" or even "dentals."

Finally, if you have a good light, you will be able to watch yourself form the first sounds of "kite" and "guy" (or the last sounds of "look" and "log") and the last sound of "song." For these sounds the back (dorsum) of your tongue touches your soft palate (velum). Accordingly, these sounds are often called "dorsovelars" or simply "velars."

Now we are ready to start our chart of English consonants:

Bilabial	Alveolar	Velar
p	t	k
b	d	g
m	n	ŋ

For all nine of these consonants there is complete stoppage in the mouth. With /m,n,ŋ/, however, we leave open a passage through the nose. Because we do so, we can protract /m/ as long as we have breath: /mmmmmmmm/. We call these three sounds "nasals." The sounds /p,t,k,b, d,g/, on the other hand, involve complete stoppage of both mouth and nose. For this reason we cannot protract them; we can only repeat them: /p-p-p-p/, and so forth. We call them "stops."

Now, what of the differences between the series /p,t,k/ and the series /b,d,g/? First of all, voice vibration accompanies the /b,d,g/, but not /p,t,k/. Try putting your fingers in your ears and saying "pie," "buy," "pie," "buy"; or "lacking," "lagging." Second, the /p,t,k/ series is more strongly articulated; when placed at the beginning of a word, a noticeable puff of air follows such a consonant. You can test the difference between "pie" and "buy" by holding a thin strip of paper or a lighted match (not both at once) in front of your lips as you pronounce the words.

One large group of consonants consists of "fricatives." These are sounds which can be protracted indefinitely and which involve audible local friction somewhere in the speech tract. Two, /f,v/, are "labiodental"; that is, we form local friction between the upper teeth and lower lip. Of these, /f/ is voiceless and strongly articulated, whereas /v/ is voiced and weakly articulated. Two more, /θ,ð/, are "interdental"; we produce these by letting the tongue go lax and flat, touching the teeth lightly and evenly all the way around, sometimes protruding between the teeth. Four others, /s,z,š,ž/, are formed with a groove running down the tongue from front to back. The groove is narrow for /s,z/, wider for /š,ž/. The last, /h/, is variously formed, depending on the nature of the following vowel.

Two more sounds, /č,ǰ/, have audible local friction; but this friction follows a complete closure. Accordingly, we classify these sounds with the "stops."

We may now add to our original chart of the consonants:

Stops:	Voiceless:	p	t	č	k	
	Voiced:	b	d	ǰ	g	
Fricatives:	Voiceless:	f	θ s	š	—	h
	Voiced:	v ð	z	ž	—	
Nasals:		m	n	—	ŋ	

Two more consonants, /w,y/, are glides to or from the positions of /u,i/, respectively.

Finally, the consonants /l,r/ fail to fit neatly into the chart we devised. They are also two of the consonants which give the most trouble to students from many language backgrounds, particularly Japanese, Korean, and Chinese. What do we know about them?

Most of the varieties of /l/ which we use have the tip of the tongue firmly against the gum ridge, and sides of the tongue pulled in so that sound may escape around it. The technical term is "lateral."

Our /r/ sound offers no problem at the end of words ("hear," "four") or between vowel and consonant ("part," "worse"), for in these positions many varieties of English omit it, or replace it with a glide toward the vowel of "but." (This glide is symbolized in Transcription 1 by /-h/). In other positions, though, the /r/ sound is unavoidable; no one leaves /r/ out of "real" or "pretty."

Many speakers of English form the /r/ sound by turning the tip of the tongue up toward the roof of the mouth *without letting it touch* the inside of the mouth anywhere. We call it a "retroflex" consonant.

For completeness the English consonants appear according to their physical characteristics on the following page.

So much for the rough inventory of English vowels and consonants. But what about the student whose language has a sound like the /s/ in "state" and another like the /t/ in "state," but who always pronounces this word so that it sounds like "estate"? This student is having trouble, not with the consonants themselves, but with the consonant group or "cluster" in which they occur. This language has no /st-/ cluster at the beginning of words. For this reason

		Bilabial	Labio-dental	Interdental	Apico-alveolar	Blade-palatal	Dorso-velar	Glottal
Stop:	Voiceless:	p			t	č	k	
	Voiced:	b			d	ǰ	g	
Fricative:	Voiceless:		f	θ	s	š		h
	Voiced:		v	ð	z	ž		
Nasal:		m			n		ŋ	

Other: w,y; r,l

you must teach clusters as well as individual consonants, and (in principle, at least) teach each cluster separately, once for each position it occupies in words. For a list of English consonant clusters see Fries' *Teaching and Learning English as a Foreign Language*, p. 17 ff.

In addition to its vowels and consonants English has other contrasting elements in its sound system. Those which we are prepared to discuss at the present time are contrasts of transition (open vs. close), stress (four levels), pitch (four levels), and phrase termination (three types).[7]

[7] Another common term for transition is "juncture." The three types of phrase termination are sometimes called "terminal contours" or "terminal junctures."

You may be familiar with the story of the chemistry student who said that the chief characteristic of nitrates is that they are cheaper than day rates. This pun turns on the fact that "nitrate" and "night rate" are pronounced with exactly the same vowels and consonants. Yet speakers of English pronounce these words differently. The difference is in the type of transition we make between the /t/ and the /r/. What we have in "nitrate" /naytreyt/ is "close transition," whereas "night rate" /nayt + reyt/ contains an "open transition." [8] We may symbolize open transition by /+/ or simply by leaving a blank space; we could just as well write "night rate" as /nayt reyt/. We also see open transition in the difference between "an aim" /an+eym/ and "a name" /a + neym/.

Differences of stress seldom form the sole difference between words. One example, however, in the speech of some people is the difference between "billow" /bílow/ and "below" /bilów/. The most important function of correct stress in English (and it *is* very important) is to help the hearer know which word goes with which other word, and how.

Each of the words /bílow/ and /bilów/ contains one syllable with the heaviest stress that English uses and one with the lightest. Intermediate levels of stress may be seen in:

We need thrêe cóats.	(′ is primary, ⌃ is secondary)
We need òur cóats.	(ˋ is tertiary)
We need sŏme cóats.	(˘ is weak)

[8] Or "plus juncture."

The four pitch levels appear in the following examples, which are numbered from 1 (low) to 4 (extra high)[9]:

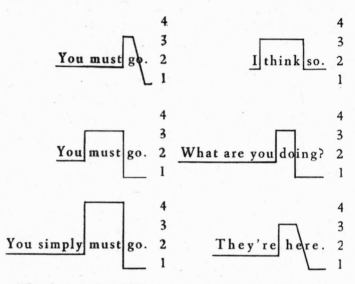

The three types of phrase termination are a little harder to illustrate clearly. We may symbolize them by /↑/, /↓/, and /→/. Gleason[10] calls them "rising," "fading," and "sustained," respectively. He describes rising as "a sudden, rapid, but short rise in pitch." Of fading he says, "A rapid trailing away of the voice into silence. Both pitch and volume decrease rapidly." The volume does not trail off so noticeably, but it seems to be comparatively sharply cut off. Sustained termination is "a sustention of the pitch ac-

[9] Some books reverse this numbering, using 1 for extra high, 4 for low.

[10] In his *Introduction to Descriptive Linguistics,* p. 46.

companied by prolongation of the last syllable of the clause and some diminishing of volume." Here are some examples:

We're here ↓

I think so ↓

I think so → but I'm not sure ↓

Are you ready → children ↑

Sunday ↑ Not ↑ Saturday ↓

Chicago is big ↑ and Detroit is → too ↓

Do you think so ↑

Two sets of teaching materials which treat pitch and stress, as well as vowels and consonants, are the Michigan *Intensive Course in English* and the books developed by the American Council of Learned Societies.

In describing the envelope into which we fit English vowels and consonants, we have discussed stress, intonation levels, and phrase terminations. We must also say a word about rhythm. There are many languages in the world which assign to every syllable just about the same amount of time. Thus, in these languages the amount of time that it takes to say a particular word or phrase is proportional to the number of syllables in it. When we hear people talking in these languages, we say they "sound like machine guns."

The rhythm of English is of another kind. In English we tend to treat our "accented" syllables in a special way, making them higher in pitch, louder in volume, and also *longer*. At the same time, we make the unstressed syllables comparatively short, so that we have a series of heavy syllables coming along at almost equal intervals, between which are any number of unstressed syllables. As a result, the length of time it takes us to say a phrase depends not so much on how many syllables the phrase contains as it does on the number of *stressed* syllables. Speakers of "machine-gun" languages might conceivably accuse us of "talking like cannons": BOOM da da BOOM da BOOM da da.

A word on the place of transcriptions. The only reason for having them at all is to make up for the shortcomings of our traditional writing system. Your student may need some set of unambiguous symbols which will remind him that "women" and "win" both have the same stressed vowel, though they are spelled differently; or that the vowel sounds of "rough," "though," and "cough" are all different, though spelled the same. Likewise, he may need a notation that will help him remember how speakers of English use pitch, stress, and juncture. And that's all a transcription is for.

If you remember this, you won't be disturbed when you find yourself using a textbook with no transcription or with very elaborate transcription or with a set of symbols quite unlike the ones on pp. 88-90. Transcription is just a memory aid. What is more important is that your students

102

listen to and imitate the whole range: vowels, consonants, pitch, stress, juncture. Otherwise they will be flirting with unintelligibility.

2. *About English Grammar*

English grammar, like the grammar of any language, is enormously complex. No one has ever described it completely. Even the partial descriptions that do exist are subject to much criticism from one group of scholars or another. Yet your effectiveness in helping people learn English depends in large part upon how skillfully you can steer your students over the hard spots in the grammar.

If English grammar is really so complicated, what hope can we offer—what help can you possibly get—from a nontechnical book like this one? We shall try to equip you with some understanding of "what grammar is about," a rough list of some very important elements in the grammar of our language, and an index which will help you find some of the grammatical information salted away in the notes in the ACLS materials and in Michigan's *Intensive Course in English*. Further than this, we can only urge you to make yourself familiar with more comprehensive works such as those listed in the bibliography.

In what we have to say about grammar we shall avoid out-and-out exposition. Instead we shall try to lead you to your own conclusions by means of a series of exercises.

a) Exercises, Set 1. The first set of exercises tries to show you how we can make statements about grammar without talking in terms of meaning. Try not to look at the "answers" on the right-hand side of the page until you have worked out your own solutions.

Directions: Give a concise description of the "sentence

structure" of the following "languages." Each line represents a different "sentence." Spend no more than ten
minutes on each section.

Language A	*Grammatical Statement*
(1) X O	"A sentence consists of an X alone
(2) X O O	or followed by one, two, or three
(3) X O O O	O's."
(4) X	

Language B	*Grammatical Statement*
(1) O X	"A sentence consists of two or
(2) O X O	three O's except that the second
(3) O O	O may be replaced by X."
(4) O O O	

Language C	*Grammatical Statement*
(1) O X	"A sentence consists of OX and
(2) O X O	may be preceded or followed by
(3) O X O O	one or two O's."
(4) O O X	
(5) O O O X	

Language D	*Grammatical Statement*
(1) M L	"This language has two classes of
(2) N K	forms. Class 1 contains M, N, O,
(3) M K	and X. Class 2 contains L, K, and
(4) O R	R. A sentence consists of a mem-
(5) X L	ber of Class 1 followed by a mem-
(6) X K	ber of Class 2."
(7) O L	
(8) N R	

b) Exercises, Set 2. In doing the second series of exercises, try to find a group of friends to work along with you.

In fact, you might even be able to use this set of problems as a party game! (In all these exercises, try not to be very original.)

(1) (*a*) Write a short sentence containing the word "house." (Each member of the group makes up his own sentence.)

(*b*) Write a sentence identical with the first except that it contains some other word in place of "house."

(*c*) Try substituting in *your* sentence the words which your friends put into *their* second sentences. List their words here (List A):

(2) Do the same with another sentence containing "small":

(*a*)

(*b*)

(*c*) (List B):

(3) Do the same with another sentence containing "understand":

(*a*)

(*b*)

(*c*) (List C):

(4) Compare the results which you found in steps (1)(c), (2)(c), and (3)(c) with the results that you get when you:

(*a*) Try to put members of List A in the sentence you used for (2).

(*b*) Try to put members of List A in the sentence that you used for (3).

(*c*) Try to put members of List B in the sentence you used for (1).

(*d*) Try to put members of List B in the sentence you used for (3).

(e) Try to put members of List C in the sentence you used for (1).

(f) Try to put members of List C in the sentence you used for (2).

(5) Now discuss the following questions and then enter your own conclusions below.

    (a) (i) Did steps (1)(c), (2)(c), or (3)(c) ever lead you to try any *impossible* substitutions?

        (ii) Why—or why not?

    (b) (i) Did any of the substitutions that you tried in (4) turn out to be possible?

        (ii) Why—or why not?

Ordinarily the results of the exercises in this set will be something like this: The substitutions in (1)(c), (2)(c), and (3)(c) will be successful. That is, they will yield "good English," though the actual ideas expressed by the sentences will sometimes be hilarious. The substitutions of (4) will, on the whole, be unsuccessful. If a few turn out to be successful, we can say it is because some English words of identical pronunciation and spelling happen to be members of two or more "parts of speech."

The words of List A can all be used in the same set of sentences. They have other privileges in common, too. For example, they can form plurals; they can occur in the phrase "of the _____." In the same way the words of List B, or the words of List C, share many privileges with one another. This is, in fact, what we mean when we say that Lists A, B, and C represent three different parts of speech, or "word classes." You will recognize that their traditional names are "nouns," "adjectives," and "verbs," respectively.

Of course, you could have replaced the words in (1), (2), and (3) with whole phrases: for example, instead of "house," you could have put "big house," "big house on the corner," "awful-looking edifice that should have been torn down years ago," and so forth. Each of these longer expressions, like the words in List A, has certain privileges in common with "house." They function like "house." We may say that List A and all these longer expressions constitute a single "function class."

Finally, notice what happens when we combine members of List B with members of List A and use a certain stress pattern: "small," "large," "pretty," "old" are possible members of List B; "house," "tree," "street," "dog" are members of List A. We may produce various combinations:

small	dog
pretty	house
old	street

We feel that there is a certain "sameness" shared by all such combinations. We may say that all examples of List B plus List A are members of the same construction.

There are of course numerous word classes in English. Some, like the ones we have already talked about, have many, many members. Others are small.

Words or constructions may combine with constructions to form larger constructions:

"The" (a word class we have not talked about) plus "house" (List A); "The house" plus "fell" (List B).

c) *Exercises, Set* 3. For the third set of exercises you will need a picture which tells a definite story. The covers of the *Saturday Evening Post* are excellent for this purpose.

This set of exercises has a two-fold purpose: to present to you, one by one, some of the most common word classes and constructions of present-day English, and to give you practice in writing within narrow restrictions of grammar and vocabulary.

(1) First of all, choose six "count nouns" that you think will be useful in telling an interesting story about your picture. A count noun is a word which ordinarily occurs in the frame "two _____s": "two *houses*," "two *cities*," "*two cups*," etc., and does not occur in "_____ is good." A "mass noun," by contrast, is one which functions like "milk" or "sugar," as in "two *cups of* milk," "three *pounds of* sugar." List your six count nouns.

(2) Write out each count noun with "a" or "an." You now have a total vocabulary of eight words.

(3) Now take the word sequence (not "construction") "This is." Write it out with all the constructions from Step (2) above. By this stage your student has a total repertoire of six complete sentences.

(4) You may now substitute "that" for "this." Total repertoire has jumped to twelve sentences. "This" and "that" are members of the same word class.

(5) Now, with no addition of new vocabulary, try switching the positions of "this"/"that" and "is." This gives you twelve brand-new sentences, different from all that have gone before. You recognize them as questions. In English this arbitrary way of signaling that we are asking a question is very important. Furthermore, it seems quite foreign to students from many language backgrounds.

(6) Add "yes" to your vocabulary.

(7) Add "it," in the sentence "It is a _____." Total repertoire is now thirty-one sentences.

108

(8) "Yes, it is." Note that we can omit the noun phrase in a short answer like this.

(9) "No." Notice that "yes" and "no" belong to a word class with only these two members.

(10) "No, it isn't."

(11) Next, add the plurals of the six count nouns in Step (1). Note that your students now have to learn that these plurals cannot follow "a" ("a house," etc.). Note also the difference in pronunciation of the plural endings in words that end with different sounds: "dish" has /dišəz/, "dog" has /dɔgz/, "duck" has /dəks/.

(12) "These are ＿＿＿＿＿s."

(13) "These" may be replaced by "those."

(14) "Is" may be replaced by "are." Note the very important fact of agreement in number among "this"/ "these," "is"/"are," "a"/"＿," and "house"/"houses." In English this is an important signal for showing which words go together as subject and verb.

(15) "They are ＿＿＿＿＿s." At this point note the extra dividend: adding no further constructions and no further vocabulary, you get eighteen new sentences of the type "Are they ＿＿＿＿＿s?" "Yes, they are"/"No, they aren't."

(16) Add "I"/"we"/"you"/"he"/"she." Note how these words pair off with "is"/"am"/"are." Use them in the sentences of Steps (1)-(15).

Now, using the picture you have chosen, write as interesting a "story" or dialogue as you can, remaining within the limits in Steps (1)-(16). An example of what others have done within these limitations is given below, in connection with a picture which shows a pair of newlyweds in a car behind a school bus:

A: Is this a bus?
B: No, it isn't. It is a car.
A: Is this a man?
B: Yes, it is.
A: Is that a man?
B: No, it isn't. It is a woman.

(17) You may now add the word "not," as used with the various forms of "be." At this point you would have to show where "not" is located relative to the verb and to other words, both in statements and in questions, and to teach use of two sets of contractions ("he's not" vs. "he isn't").

(18) Add three qualifying adjectives. A qualifying adjective is one that fits into the frame "It's a very ———— thing." Choose adjectives that will help you make your story interesting. At this point you may also add a seventh count noun.

(19) Next, add the construction "this"/"that" plus a count noun. True, you have already had all these words, but until now "this" and "that" have only occurred alone as subjects of sentences.

(20) Add the construction adjective plus count noun and put "a"/"an" before it to form a more complex construction.

(21) Use the adjectives alone after forms of "be." ("This house is *white*," etc.)

(22) Use "the" with count nouns, or count nouns plus adjectives.

(23) Use a prepositional phrase (e.g., *"in* a basket") after a form of "be."

(24) Choose two prepositions which you think will

110

make your story interesting. (Some common prepositions are "in," "on," "at," "to," "for," "by," "under.")

(25) Add the word "and." Notice that this word joins units of several types: adjectives ("big" and "red"), count nouns with "a"/"an"/"the" ("the house" and "the yard"), prepositional phrases ("in the yard" and "around the house"), and so forth.

(26) Now write a series of questions with "where": "Where is the house?" and the like.

(27) Next, write some sentences of the form "There is a _____ on the _____." Notice that the word "there" as used in these sentences is always unstressed, unlike the word which is spelled the same way in "There he is."

(28) Write some sentences containing "mine," "yours," "his," "hers," "its," "theirs," "ours."

(29) Write some sentences containing "my," "your," "his," "her," "its," "their," "our."

(30) You may now start using possessive forms of nouns. Three things to remember: first, there is a variation in pronunciation similar to the one we noticed for the plurals in Step (11); second, the use of the apostrophe in writing possessives is a separate teaching problem; third, many nouns which stand for inanimate things use a prepositional phrase with "of _____" rather than the possessive form with "_____'s."

(31) Write a sentence of the form "The _____ is _____ -ing now."

(32) Choose any four verbs. Note that at this stage they will have to be "intransitive" verbs; that is, they will have to be verbs that don't need to have nouns following them. Some intransitive verbs are "work," "walk," "talk,"

"sleep," "smile." Using whatever you can from the vocabulary and grammar in Steps (1)-(30), write sentences with these verbs. Now write the most interesting dialogue or commentary you can about the picture you have chosen. Here is a further example:

This is a bus. It is a large bus. These are students. The students are in the large bus. They are not in the car. They are laughing.

This is a man. That is a woman. This is a new car. These are new suitcases. They are in the car. The man and the woman are in the new car. The man is driving. The man and woman are happy.

(33) Write a sentence of the form "The ———— has been ———— -ing." Note that the choice of "has"/"have" depends on your choice of singular or plural count noun as subject.

(34) Choose two more intransitive verbs and use them in sentences like those in Steps (31) and (33).

(35) Now choose four more verbs—transitive ones this time. Some verbs that are usually transitive are "see," "hear," "understand," "throw." Write sentences using these verbs with count nouns as their direct objects.

(36) Now, by reversing the order of subject and certain auxiliary verbs, notice that you can create "yes"-"no" questions: "Has he been ———— -ing?" "Is he ———— -ing now?"

(37) Use "not" with the statements and questions on Steps (31), (33), (36). Notice where you have to locate "not" in each type of sentence. This placing of "not" is hard for many students from other language backgrounds.

(38) Choose any three time expressions—words or

groups of words—that are compatible with "He is ———
-ing." (You have already had one: "now.") Use them with
your stock of verbs. Make the time expressions as long and
complex as you like, but remember that you may not alter
them by one word in the remainder of this exercise! For
example, "at this very moment."

(39) Choose any three time expressions that are compatible with "He has been ——— -ing"; e.g., "since you
were here last week."

(40) Now write some sentences with the so-called
"simple present" form of some of your verbs. Notice the
differences in meaning signaled by such differences in form
as "He walks to school (every day)" vs. "He is walking to
school (now)." Note also the choice of "walk"/"walks,"
depending on what word is subject of the verb.

(41) Choose three time expressions compatible with
the simple present forms of verbs.

(42) Change some statements with simple present
verbs into questions that can be answered by "yes" or "no."
What formal changes did you make in the statement to
signal this difference in meaning?

(43) Do the same with "not" plus some "simple
present" sentences. The changes you have made in Steps
(42) and (43) are among the most arbitrary changes in
English and are hard for almost all types of students.

(44) Choose three more verbs.

(45) Choose three two-word verbs. These verbs
should have stress on the second element. Some examples
are "stand up," "sit down," "set down," "put away."

(46) Choose five more prepositions.

(47) Write some sentences with the "going-to"
future: "He is going to wake up," etc. Notice how you

113

form negatives and "yes"/"no" questions with this type of verb phrase.

(48) Choose three time expressions that you can use with the "going-to" future.

(49) Choose five new count nouns, two new conjunctions ("or" and "but," probably), and six new qualifying adjectives.

(50) Write a new version of your story or dialogue.

(51) Add the question words "Who?" "What?" "When?" Notice how they affect the order of subject and verb and how they require "do"/"does" with the simple present form.

(52) Now introduce the simple past tense, with its question patterns and negative patterns. Notice the different pronunciation of the "regular" past ending with "walk" /wɔkt/ "show"/šowd/, "pat"/pætəd/. This should remind you of the plural endings we talked about in connection with Step (11). Remember also that many of the most common and most useful verbs form the past tense in an irregular way: "run" has /ræn/, "send" has /sent/, "put" has /put/.

Your student has to learn each of these forms separately. It's a good idea *not* to have him just practice saying "run, ran; send, sent; put, put." Instead let him practice them in short but realistic sentences. By so doing he will also be practicing some of the rules which govern the way each verb is used in sentences: "He runs every afternoon." "He ran yesterday." "He sends some money every week; he sent it yesterday."

(53) Choose three time expressions that will go with the past forms of your verbs and will also contribute to your story.

114

(54) Write some sentences in which you use "can" with the simple form of some of the verbs. Note that "he," "she," "it," do *not* require a form *"cans."* "Can," when used in this way sometimes is called a "modal." Notice how modals are used in questions or with "not." This fact about word order is difficult for most students.

(55) Choose three more verbs.

(56) Choose two more modals. Some common modals are "will," "could," "may," "must," "might," "would" "should."

(57) Choose three qualifying adverbs. These should be words that can be used with "very" in sentences like "He did it very _____." ("rapidly," "well," "poorly," "cheer-fully")

(58) Add numerals from one to ten. These ten words are unrelated in form.

(59) Add numerals from sixteen to nineteen. Notice how they are related in form to certain numerals from Step (58).

(60) Add numerals from eleven to fifteen. Why do these present a special problem not found in Step (59)?

(61) Add numerals from twenty to one hundred.

(62) Now add the words "some" and "any," pronounced with weak stress: "We need some paper"; "do you have any paper?" but *not* "Any paper will do."

(63) Add "also," and "too" when it is used like "also." You are *not yet* authorized to use it with adjectives or adverbs, as in "too big," "too slowly."

(64) Add stressed "here"/"there." ("Here is your coat," etc.)

(65) Write some sentences of the form "The _____ has _____ the _____." ("The dog has torn the

curtain.") Write questions and negative statements with this kind of phrasal verb.

Notice that for many common verbs your students now have to learn a third form ("write," "wrote," *"written"*), whereas for many others no new form is needed ("wait," "waited").

(66) Choose three time expressions that will go with the verb forms of Step (65) and will help your story.

(67) Add "many" and use it in a few sentences.

(68) Add "every" and "no," as in "every child," "no child."

(69) Choose three mass nouns which you can use in talking about your picture. (See the first step for a discussion of count nouns.) Some frequent mass nouns are "water," "food," "work." Note that

although we say:	we usually say:
Count Noun	*Mass Noun*
a dog	(some) water
some dogs	some water
two dogs	two quarts of water
a few dogs	a little water
many dogs	much water

(70) Add "much" to your vocabulary.

(71) Choose three "frequency adverbs." Some of the most common of these are "often," "seldom," "sometimes," "never," "always." As a group they are distinguished from other adverbs by the position which they frequently occupy between auxiliary verb and main verb: "I have *never* forgotten your birthday."

(72) Now write a few sentences using "marked in-

116

finitives"—"to" plus the simple form of the verb: "I need to buy an alarm clock."

(73) Add four mass nouns, four count nouns, four verbs, and four qualifying adjectives.

(74) Now—write as interesting a story as possible relating to your picture. For example:

A man and his wife are driving along the road very slowly in their new car. They have been married for only a few minutes and have just started on a long trip. They have packed their suitcases and put them in the car. The suitcases are new; the car is also new. The man bought the car only a few days ago.

The man seldom drives slowly but now his car is behind this large bus and he cannot pass it. Whenever the bus stops the car has to stop. While the bus is stopped a car may not pass. The man has to drive slowly.

Many of the children are standing up to see the man and his wife. They have been sitting down in the bus but now they are standing up. They are very curious. The man and his wife are not looking at the children. The children are laughing at them, but the man and his wife do not care. They are thinking about the long trip. They are very happy. The children are happy, too.

The steps which we have just outlined represent one sequence in which this much of English grammar might actually be introduced to a group of students. We are *not,* however, putting it forward as the only, or even the best, such sequence.

d) Dealing with mistakes in grammar. Now, all this talk about grammar naturally leads us into further talk about grammatical *errors.* In dealing with our students' mistakes we need to begin by drawing a distinction between errors

117

of two sorts, both of which are commonly labeled "grammatical." The first, which we shall call "intralingual," rests on a difference which sets apart some speakers of a language from others. For example:

> He doesn't understand.
> versus
> He don't understand.

Where such differences of usage exist, we often associate one of the alternative expressions with superior educational or social status. [11] Another type of intralingual difference may have geographical as well as social connotations: "skillet," "frying pan," "spider"; "seesaw," "teeter-totter"; "bag," "sack," "poke," etc.

A second category of grammatical errors includes expressions which no adult native speaker of the language would use:

> He no understand.
> You have watch, yes?
> Two person is arrive.

These we shall call "nonnative"; they interfere with intelligibility much more seriously than do intralingual errors.

Now, we want our students to learn a form of English which is not only intelligible but also as widely acceptable as possible. That is, we try to help them avoid the intralingual as well as the nonnative errors. But it should be obvious that the nonnative problems are far more fundamental than the intralingual ones and for this reason

[11] Fries, in his *American English Grammar*, discusses these differences in a very helpful way.

118

must receive greater emphasis and a larger share of the time spent in grammar drill.

If you are a typical native speaker of English, without linguistic training, you may be surprised at the kinds of mistakes your students make: the right way seems so obvious to us and the wrong way so strained and unnecessary. Remember, however, that most, if not all, of your students' nonnative errors may be traced to the ways in which their language differs from English; by and large, speakers of a given language will make the same recurrent errors, whereas speakers of another language may have quite a different set of problems.

We may now further subdivide our nonnative problems into two groups. We shall illustrate both varieties by reference to a single (correct) English sentence: "The young couple across the street usually give their baby a bottle on the train at night, don't they?"

(1) *Errors of word order*

    (*a*) "They their baby a bottle give."

        Comment: The student's native language may regularly put the verb last. Or it may allow the verb to appear anywhere in the sentence. But in English the order subject-verb-object in statements is very firmly fixed; accordingly, violating this order constitutes a serious error.

    (*b*) "The couple young usually give . . ." or "The across the street couple . . ."

        Comment: In English single-word modifiers of nouns almost always precede them, whereas modifiers which contain clauses or prepositional phrases follow them.

    (*c*) ". . . give to their baby a bottle . . ." or ". . . give a bottle their baby . . ."

Comment: The relative order of "baby" and "bottle" in this sentence depends on using or omitting "to" (or vice versa).

(2) *Interdependent elements in the sentence*

(*a*) "They gives their baby a bottle . . ."

Comment: The "gives"-form of the verb is used only with third person singular subjects, whereas other subjects take the "give"-form. Why should this be so? The reasons are historical, not logical.

(*b*) "The young couple . . . give his baby a bottle . . ."

Comment: Learning to use the right pronoun with the right antecedent is a problem for all students, but particularly for those whose native languages fail to provide them with a precedent for differentiating among pronouns as we do. Some languages, for example, have a single pronoun for which we have "he" and "she" or for which we have "he," "she," and "it."

(*c*) "They usually give their baby a bottle at night, isn't it?"

Comment: This error, preposterous as it sounds to many natives, actually is not uncommon. The "they" of the correct form depends on the choice of subject, whereas the "don't" depends on the constitution of the verb phrase: "They *can* give . . . , *can't* they?" "They *will* give . . . , *won't* they?" and so on. Finally, the use of "-n't" depends partly on the presence or absence of a negative in the main clause: we don't usually say "they don't give . . . , don't they?"

120

In many languages it is quite simple to form these little "tag questions," for they are invariable in form. Witness Spanish *"no es verdad,"* German *"nicht wahr,"* French *"n'est-ce pas,"* Japanese *"ne."* And it's this same simplicity of these languages at this point which causes their native speakers to have so much difficulty with the more complex English pattern.

(d) "They have given their baby a bottle last night . . ."

Comment: The dependence here is between the verb form and the time expression. When your students have trouble using tenses correctly, concentrate on pointing out this interdependence and providing drills on it. That will be more helpful than having your students memorize rules or providing them with a set of statements that are supposed to "define the meaning" of each tense.

(e) ". . . at the night . . ."

Comment: Many languages lack anything comparable to our "a," "an," "the." Even for speakers of languages like Armenian or German, which do have comparable elements, the decision as to which English article to use—if any—is a ticklish one. Although the problem is only partially one of interdependent sentence elements, we shall discuss it here.

The patterning of these little words is so complex that until now no one has succeeded in formulating a set of rules which will enable

121

the nonnative to predict with *complete* accuracy just when he should use "a," "the," or no article at all.

Thus, we may say:	but never say:
at night	"at morning"
at noon	"at afternoon"
at school	"at post office"
at home	"at house"
in the night	"at the noon"
in the morning	"at the midnight"
in the Bronx	"in the Brooklyn"

In the face of such arbitrary restrictions as these, your student must simply practice doing things one way with one list of words, another way with another.

(f) "They talk their baby at night . . ."

Comment: Another common source of trouble is the little group of words called prepositions: "in," "on," "at," "to," "for," "with," and the rest.

Sometimes the difference between two prepositions can be set forth fairly clearly in terms of their meanings. But in those cases in which your student repeatedly makes the same mistakes in handling prepositions, you may be fairly sure that the two (or more) prepositions which he is confusing sometimes have the same translation in his language, or perhaps that the two correspond to a pair of elements in his language in the following way:

"to"		"for"
X		Y

ENGLISH

STUDENT'S LANGUAGE

That is, in *most* instances "to" corresponds to X and "for" to Y, so the student uses "to" in English wherever he would have X in his own language. This leads him to errors in those expressions which are represented by the shaded portion of the diagram.

The choice of a preposition often depends on the identity of the words with which it is associated. Thus, "dependent *on*," "independent *of*"; "look *at*," "listen *to*." We cannot often do justice to such awkward facts with statements based on *meanings*. And even when we can, the student learns mainly by memorizing the examples, not the rules.

PART IV

"What Now?"

We hope that the general ideas which we set forth in Part I of this handbook are now a part of your thinking about language and language-teaching, that you have found some useful ideas among the teaching suggestions in Part II, and that you have absorbed the facts about English which we have listed in Part III. In these few paragraphs of Part IV we shall try to summarize Parts I–III by answering the question "What now?"

"What now?" Now you have a start in the field of teaching English as a foreign language, but as we have said several times, it is only a start. Your reading and your study should continue.

"What now?" Now you are aware of the twin problems of motivation and control. Most of what we have said in this handbook has borne on one or the other of these problems. Motivation is concerned with everything you do to make textbook, classroom, class, and yourself as pleasant as possible—everything you do to increase and maintain your students' desire to learn English. Yet strong motivation by itself may lead to frustration and defeat if the students are not brought constantly into contact with the language, or if their contact with the language leads them to try too much too soon, so that they become confused.

Now you are ready to apply what you have read. The

real test of the value of this handbook is likely to be the degree to which it helps you adapt for your own students the textbooks or other materials that you have at your disposal. Before you can adapt intelligently, you must be aware of the units which make up the language: these we have sketched in Part III. We hope that after going through the exercises in Part III several times you will be able to choose, write, or rewrite basic selections which will be within the limits of grammar and vocabulary that your students can handle. We hope that, given a suitable basic selection, you will have found, in other parts of this handbook and in some of the readings which we have suggested, many ideas for devising, revising, or supplementing the drills which must carry the students smoothly from basic selection to free composition. Finally, we hope that you have discovered in these pages a hint of the combined fun, hard work, and profound satisfaction that can be yours when you are helping people learn English.

BIBLIOGRAPHY

With the exception of a few extremely important publications to which we had no occasion to refer in the text, the following bibliography confines itself to those items mentioned in Parts I–III.

Agard, Frederick B., *et al. El Inglés Hablado.* New York: Henry Holt and Co., 1953. This is one of a series of courses prepared under the auspices of the American Council of Learned Societies for persons of various language backgrounds. This version is in Spanish, for speakers of Spanish. The materials are carefully sequenced. Phonetic transcription covers stress, intonation, and terminal features, as well as vowels and consonants. The Spanish version of these materials is the only one published commercially so far. Other versions have been prepared for speakers of Persian, Indonesian, Serbo-Croatian, Korean, Chinese, Greek, and Turkish.

Allen, Virginia French. *People in Livingston.* New York: Thomas Y. Crowell Co., 1953.

Cochran, Anne. *Modern Methods of Teaching English as a Foreign Language.* United Board for Christian Colleges in China, 1952. Reprinted 1954 by Educational Services, Inc., Washington, D. C. A broad and impartial survey of theories, methods, readings, and teaching materials. Has good bibliography.

Cornelius, E. T. *Teaching English.* Washington Publications, 3915 Military Road, N. W., Washington 15, D. C., 1955. An excellent summary of the objectives, techniques, problems, equipment, and preparation of the teacher of English as a second language.

Much attention is given to the assumptions and the attitudes which the teacher brings to his work.

Dale, Edgar. *Audio-visual Methods in Teaching.* New York: The Dryden Press, Inc., 1954. Not written especially for language teachers, but a thorough treatment of many techniques which we can use.

El Paso City Schools. *A Manual of Materials, Aids, and Techniques for the Teaching of Spanish to English-Speaking Children.* El Paso: 1952.

English Language Research, Inc. *Learning the English Language.* Boston: Houghton Mifflin Co., 1945.

English Language Teaching. A journal published by the British Council, London. Contains many useful articles and editorials.

Fries, Charles C. *American English Grammar.* New York: Appleton-Century-Crofts, Inc., 1940.

————. *Teaching and Learning English as a Foreign Language.* Ann Arbor: University of Michigan Press, 1947. A classic in the field. Includes samples of material developed prior to 1947 at the English Language Institute of the University of Michigan.

————. *The Structure of English.* New York: Harcourt, Brace and Co., 1952. Valuable not only for the facts it contains, but also for the approach which it illustrates. Written for the educated layman.

————, *et. al. An Intensive Course in English.* Ann Arbor: University of Michigan Press, 1953. A revision of the earlier *Intensive Course in English for Latin American Students.* The new course, like its predecessor, has been constructed especially for speakers of Spanish. Different volumes cover different aspects of the course: *Patterns of English Sentences, Cumulative Pattern Practices, English Pronunciation,* and *Lessons in Vocabulary.*

Gauntlett, John O. *Basic Principles of English Language Teaching.* Sanseido, Japan: 195(2).

Gleason, H. A. *An Introduction to Descriptive Linguistics.* New York: Henry Holt and Co., 1955. For the educated layman, an excellent summary of the linguistic science upon which many of the other items in this bibliography are based.

Gurrey, Percival. *Teaching English as a Foreign Language.* London:

Longmans, Green and Co., Inc., 1955. A very fine little book which contains clear discussions of several methods and description of many specific techniques you can use.

Hansen, G. F. *A Guide for the Teaching of French in the Elementary Schools.* Washington: U. S. Government Printing Office, 1952.

Hornsby, Albert S. *A Guide to Patterns and Usage in English.* London: Oxford University Press, 1954. Contains much useful detail, and also serves as a handy summary of the terms and symbols found in *English Language Teaching,* and in many parts of the English-speaking world.

————. Gatenby, E. V., and Wakefield, H. *The Advanced Learner's Dictionary of Current English.* London: Oxford University Press, 1948. Contains many examples of the more common ways in which each word is used.

Jespersen, Otto. *How to Teach a Foreign Language.* London: Longmans, Green and Co., Inc., 1940.

Kenyon, John S., and Knott, Thomas A. *A Pronouncing Dictionary of American English.* Springfield, Massachusetts: G. & C. Merriam Co., 1949.

Kitchin, A. T., and Allen, V. F. *Reader's Digest Readings in English as a Second Language* (two vols.) Pleasantville, New York: Reader's Digest, 1953.

Lado, Robert. *Annotated Bibliography for Teachers of English as a Foreign Language.* Washington: U. S. Government Printing Office, 1955. Comprehensive and extremely useful.

Language Learning. A journal of applied linguistics published at the University of Michigan, Ann Arbor, 1948————. Valuable for all teachers of foreign languages.

McKenzie, A. P. *Materials for Standard English Courses.* Tokyo, Japan: International Christian University, no date.

Newmark, Maxim, ed. *Twentieth Century Modern Language Teaching.* New York: Philosophical Library, Inc., 1948.

Palmer, Harold E. *The Teaching of Oral English.* London: Longmans, Green and Co., Inc., 1940.

Prator, C. *Manual of American English Pronunciation for Adult Foreign Students.* Berkeley: University of California Press, 1951.

Richards, Ivor A., and Gibson, Christine. *Learning Basic English.* New York: W. W. Norton and Co., Inc., 1945.

————. *English Through Pictures*. New York: Pocket Books, Inc., 1952.

Rojas, Pauline M., *et al*. *Fries American English Series*. Boston: D. C. Heath and Co., 1952.

San Diego Public Schools. *Handbook for the Teaching of Spanish in Elementary Grades*. San Diego: 1952.

Thomas, C. K. *An Introduction to the Phonetics of American English*. New York: The Ronald Press Co., 1947.

Thorndike-Barnhart Comprehensive Desk Dictionary. New York: Doubleday and Co., Inc., 1951. Also a pocket edition, paperbound.

Thorndike, Edward L. *Thorndike Century Senior Dictionary*. Chicago: Scott, Foresman and Co., 1941.

———— and Lorge, Irving. *The Teacher's Word Book of 30,000 Words*. New York: Teachers College Bureau of Publications, 1944.

Trager, G. L., and Smith, H. L. *Outline of English Structure*. Studies in Linguistics Occasional Paper No. 3. Norman, Oklahoma: Battenberg Press, 1951. Is influencing many materials being produced today. Difficult reading for the uninitiated, however. For a simpler exposition of a similar analysis, see Gleason.

Welmers, W. E. *Spoken English as a Foreign Language*. Washington: American Council of Learned Societies, 1953. The teachers' manual to accompany the ACLS materials.

West, Michael. *The New Method Readers*. London: Longmans, Green and Co., Inc., 1945.

———— and Endicott, James. *The New Method English Dictionary*. London: Longmans, Green and Co., Inc., 1953.

APPENDIX

In our discussion of grammar and ways of teaching it, we have spoken of the enormous complexity of the grammatical system of English—or of any language, for that matter. The index which follows is one which I made up for my own use, to help me locate the grammatical information distributed throughout three of the most reliable and up-to-date sets of teaching materials. If you can obtain access to any of these three books, you can make use of the index in the same way.

The three books are:

1. *Structural Notes and Corpus* (SNC), indexed by page numbers. This is the "general form" on the basis of which the ACLS materials were written. It is not for public sale, but we list it here because it is all in English, and you may be able to get a look at a copy.

2. *El Inglés Hablado* (IH), indexed by paragraphs. This is the Spanish version of SNC. If you can read Spanish at all, this edition has the advantages of being available commercially and of containing more notes than SNC. "Ap." refers to the appendix of this book.

3. *Patterns of English Sentences* (PES), indexed by lesson and section numbers. PES is one of the four volumes in Michigan's new *Intensive Course in English*.

This index makes little pretense to completeness or consistency; nevertheless, I hope you will find it helpful. Here is an example of the kind of information which it can help you assemble. The facts presented in the notes indexed under DEFINITE ARTICLE may be summarized as follows:

ARTICLE, DEFINITE ("the"): The definite article occurs ordinarily with the weakest degree of stress. Unlike corresponding words in some other languages, it does not change form to agree with nouns in number, gender, or case; but it does have different pronunciations depending on whether the following word begins with a vowel or a consonant sound.

A noun used with the definite article refers to something already mentioned or at least known about. Articles are used differently with mass nouns and with count nouns (see p. 108). When the superlative form of an adjective or a possessive pronoun precedes a noun, you almost always find the definite article preceding the adjective.

The definite article may be used with plural count nouns, of course, but not when the plural count noun refers to the entire class of things for which the noun stands: "I hate cats."

The article is not used before the names of hours in telling time, as it is in Spanish. Neither is it used before the names of certain daily activities: "at breakfast."

The above are only a few of the facts that your students need to know about "the" and to embed in their system of English habits. None of these facts will strike you as particularly new or surprising. But the point is that these are facts that your students need, stated in a form in which they can make almost direct use of them; it is not easy for a speaker of English to bring these facts to his consciousness on the spur of the moment or to phrase them as clearly as you will find them in the books we have indexed.

a/an, See ARTICLE, INDEFI-
   NITE
a lot of, IH 67.2

about, IH 46.5, 57.1, 61.2
ADJECTIVES: SNC 46, 47,
   72; IH 22:3, 77.1c, 82.2,

87.5; PES 1.2b, 4.3, 7.3, 13.2, 15.2

ADVERBIALS [1]: SNC 70, 71f, 84, 94, 95f, 97, 97; IH 32.1, 32.3, 42.2, 42.3, 42.7, 51.1, 52.8, 57.6c, 57.7, 77.3b-d, 87.4; PES 3.1, 3.2, 3.3, 16.2a

ADVERBS: SNC 97; IH 42.3a, 42.5, 52.2, 57.6, 62.6, 67.2h, 81.3, 87.5; PES 9.1a, b, 15.2

advise, IH 77.4e

afraid, IH 76.4

after: IH 66.5, 72.1, 72.2, 87.4a; PES 16.2b

ago, IH 52.8

all, IH 77.2

along, IH 66.5

already: IH 57.6; PES 19.2

always: IH 82.3a; PES 2.2a

any: IH 62.1; PES 5.4

anymore, PES 19.2

ARTICLE, DEFINITE: SNC 46, 60, 82, 82, 96; IH 22.2, 56.11, 67.1, 72.2a, 82.2a; PES 1.2b

ARTICLE, INDEFINITE: SNC 60, 82, 82, 96; IH 27.1, 51.6, 62.1, 67.5f, 92.1; PES 1.2a, 6.1a

as: IH 92.4; PES 15.1a, b

ask, PES 8.1a

at: SNC 84; IH 56.7, 67.1, 87.4

bad, IH 87.5b

be: SNC 24, 33, 36, 47, 50, 61, 62, 72, 80, 84, 97; IH 12.2, 17.2, 17.6c, 22.4b, 22.8, 32.4d, 36.1, 37.4, 42.2c, 42.5b, 51.6, 52.7d, 52.7e, 62.3, 62.5a, 72.5a, 77.4f, 92.4c, 92.5a, Ap. 2.1; PES

1.1d, 3.2, 3.4, 4.2a, 5.1, 19.1

beat: SNC 102; IH 46.2

because, IH 87.3

before: IH 72.2, 87.4a; PES 16.2

belong, IH 86.2

better, IH 57.4

blow, IH 96.1

body, IH 87.6a

by: IH 77.3, 82.4; PES 12.3a, 12.3b

can: SNC 35; IH 17.4; PES 11.1

catch, IH 66.5

CLAUSES, DEPENDENT, PES 16.1

clean, IH 61.4

come: SNC 73, 95, 97; IH 32.4c, 42.2c, 42.5b, 66.5, 71.4, 96.2

COMPARISONS: IH 92.4; PES 15.2

COMPOSITE VERBS: SNC 95; IH 42.3; PES 12.1

CONJUNCTIONS: IH 52.3; PES 16.2b

CONTRACTIONS: SNC 23, 25, 33, 34, 62, 68, 83; IH 12.2, 12.4c, d, e, 17.2g, 17.4d, 22.4c, 22.6, 22.9c, d, 26.2, 27.3a, 31.1, 37.4, 42.1b, 46.4, 47.4, 52.4, 62.2d, 62.3c, 72.4a, 92.3, Ap. 1.2, Ap. 4; PES 1.1b, 5.2, 18.1, 18.3

cost: SNC 84; IH 37.7a

could, IH 72.4

COUNT NOUNS: SNC 60, 82, 96; IH 27.1, 37.1a, 57.3d, 67.2a; PES 6.1a

couple, IH 77.2

[1] Including prepositional phrases.

DEMONSTRATIVES: SNC 47, 82, 83, 96; IH 22.5, 37.2c, 37.3, 42.5, 67.5f
depend, IH 56.6
DERIVATION, IH 51.3
different: IH 91.4; PES 15.1a
do: SNC 24, 36, 48, 50, 62, 71, 94; IH 12.4, 17.5d, 22.8, 22.9d, f, 27.2h, 27.3, 27.4, 32.2b, 42.1, 52.7c, 62.2b, 82.1, Ap. 2.3; PES 2.1a, 2.1c, 3.3, 3.4, 4.1, 5.2, 5.3, 9.3, 13.1b
down, IH 56.9
during, PES 16.2a

each, IH 77.2, 82.5, 92.2
eat: SNC 85; IH 37.7d
enough, PES 13.3
ever: IH 82.3c; PES 2.2b
every, IH 87.6a
expect, IH 77.4e, 81.5
explain, PES 8.1a

fact, IH 82.4
feel, IH 81.1, 81.3
few, PES 6.1b
fill, IH 86.1
find: SNC 85; IH 37.7d, 57.7c, 61.5, 77.1b
finish, IH 72.5a
fit, IH 86.1
for: SNC 95; IH 42.2d, 52.6c, d, 57.6, 81.5; PES 8.1c, 12.2a, 13.2, 16.2a, 18.1
forget, IH 61.2
freeze, IH 96.1
from: SNC 95; IH 42.2b, c; PES 15.1a
furniture, IH 51.3

get: SNC 73, 9b; IH 32.4b, 52.6c, 71.1, 76.5, 92.5b

give: IH 56.8; PES 8.1b
glad, IH 77.4b
go: SNC 73, 97; IH 32.4c, 42.5b, 71.4; PES 5.1
going, IH 67.3
good, IH 87.5b

had, PES 18.3
half, IH 76.3, 77.2
has, PES 18.1
have: SNC 25, 50, 62, 71, 73; IH 12.4, 22.8c, 22.9g, 27.2g, 32.2b, 32.4c, 46.4, 52.7e, 57.5, 62.2a, 77.4d, Ap. 2.2; PES 1.1d, 2.1b, 18.1
he: SNC 34; IH 17.3; PES 1.1e, 2.1c
hear, IH 76.2
her: SNC 48; IH 22.6c; PES 13.4
here: IH 42.5a; PES 3.1
him: SNC 48; IH 22.6b; PES 13.4
hope, IH 81.5
house, IH 76.3
how: SNC 33; IH 17.1, 46.5, 57.3c, 57.3d; PES 9.1, 12.3b

if, IH 52.3
IMPERATIVE: SNC 35, 19, 84; IH 17.5b, 22.7, 37.5; PES 7.1
in: SNC 70; IH 32.1a, 82.4, 86.1; PES 12.2b
INDEFINITE COMPOUNDS, IH 87.6
INFINITIVE, MARKED: IH 62.2, 77.4; PES 13.1, 13.4, 16.2b
inside, IH 87.1
INTERROGATIVES: SNC 33; IH 17.1, 57.2, 57.3, 57.5f. 57.7, 62.5d; PES 4.1, 5.1

INTONATION[2]: SNC vii, 4, 17, 30, 32, 44, 45, 68, 79, 80f; SNC 24, 25, 33, 35, 50, 84; IH p. xii, 2.5, 2.6, 2.7, 9.4, 9.5, 9.6, 9.7, 9.8, 12.2b, d, 12.4d, e, 12.5, 15.6, 15.7, 17.1f, 17.2f, 17.4c, 22 F 1 (2, 3,) 22.9, 35.6, 35.7, 52.3, 52.7f, 55.4, 65.5, 65.6, 67.2h, 75.4, 80.3, 85.5, 90.6, 96.7, 97.1

is, SNC 34, 61

it: SNC 34, 48; IH 17.3, 32.1d, 72.6, 77.4g, 96.3; PES 1.1e, 2.1c, 14.1a

just: SNC 97; IH 42.6, 81.3

keep: SNC 84; IH 37.7b

know: SNC 73; IH 32.4c, 41.6, 57.7c

least, PES 15.3

let's: SNC 49; IH 22.7b; PES 7.1

like (v): IH 31.4, 62.2a, 62.2e, 72.5b, 76.7, 77.4e; PES 4.2a

like (prep.): PES 15.1a; IH 81.3

little, PES 6.1b

look, IH 56.7, 81.3

lot, PES 6.1b

make: SNC 85; IH 37.7c

man: SNC 80; IH 36.3

many: IH 57.3d, 67.2; PES 6.1b, 6.4

MASS NOUNS: SNC 60, 82; IH 27.1, 37.1, 57.3d, 67.2; PES 6.1a

may, PES 11.1

me: SNC 48; IH 22.6a; PES 13.4

meet, IH 41.6

MODALS: SNC 35, 50, 61; IH 17.4, 17.5c, 22.8, 22.9e, f, 27.2f, 52.4, 57.4, 67.6, 72.4, 92.3, *Ap.* 3

much: IH 57.3d, 67.2, 92.4a; PES 6.1b, 6.4

must, IH 92.3

nap, IH 61.6

near: SNC 84; IH 37.6b

NEGATIVE: SNC 24, 24, 25, 83, 84, 94; IH 12.2, 12.4b, c, e, 17.4d, 17.5d, 27.3a, 37.4d, 42.1b, 52.2, 52.7b, 57.5f, 62.1a, 62.2b, 62.5b, 67.2f, 87.6, 92.4c; PES 1.1c, 2.1d, 5.2, 5.3, 5.4, 6.4, 11.1b, 11.2a, 13.1c, 18.1, 19.2

never: IH 82.3c; PES 2.2b, 5.3

none, PES 6.4

not: SNC 24, 25, 83, 94, 9; IH 12.2, 12.4c, 17.4d, 17.5c, 27.3a, 37.4, 42.1b, 57.5f, 62.3c, 62.5b, 72.4a, 54.4b, 57.4b, 82.3c, 92.3; PES 1.1c, 5.2, 5.3, 13.1c, 18.1

NOUN ADJUNCT: SNC 85; IH 37.8; PES 4.3

NOUN-NOUN COMPOUND: SNC 85; IH 37.8; PES 4.3

NOUN-NOUN PHRASE: SNC 85; PES 4.3

NOUNS: SNC 45, 46, 46, 50, 60, 70, 72, 80, 85, 96, 97, 104; IH 12.1a, 22.1, 27.1,

---

[2] See also *English Pronounciation*, in the revised *Intensive Course in English*, from the English Language Institute of the University of Michigan.

32.1a, 37.1, 37.8, 42.5b, 47.1, 51.6, 67.2, 67.4, 67.5d-f, 72.5d, 77.2, 77.4d, 87.2, 97.3; PES 1.2a, 4.3
now, IH 62.6, 87.6a
NUMERALS: SNC 82, 91; IH 37.1b, 41.2, 41.3, 67.1

OBJECTS OF VERBS, IH 52.6, 77.4e
o'clock, IH 67.1
of: SNC 82; IH 37.1b, 52.1, 67.5f, 77.2a, 87.1a; PES 14.2
off, SNC 96
often, PES 2.2a
on: SNC 70, 71; IH 32.1b, 56.6, 71.1
one: SNC 96; IH 42.4, 87.6a; PES 14.3b
other: SNC 50, 96; IH 22.9a, 92.1, 92.2; PES 7.3
out, IH 77.1b, 86.1, 96.2
outside, IH 87.1

pack, IH 51.2
past, IH 72.1
people: SNC 46; IH 22.1e
PERSON—NUMBER IN VERBS: SNC 24, 33, 48, 61, 62; IH 12.2, 12.4a, 17.2, 17.5e, 22.1e, 22.4b, 22.5d, 27.2a, 67.5e, 72.6c; PES 11.1b, 1.1b, 1.2b, 2.1b, 2.1c, 3.2, 3.3, 7.2
pick, IH 71.1
place, IH 77.4d
plan, IH 62.2a
please, PES 7.1
plural, PES 6.1b, 6.2, 7.3
PLURALS: SNC 45, 46, 60, 80, 82, 83, 96; IH 22.1, 27.1d, 36.3, 37.3, 42.4c, 61.1, 67.4d, 67.5c, 81.2, 92.1; PES

1.2a, 7.1
PLUS JUNCTURE: SNC 4, 5, 6, 11, 15, 16, 34, 46; IH 8.2, 8.7, 12.2d, 12.4d, 17.2e, 22.1d, 22.6, 22.9d, e, 37.4b, 57.5b, 87.6a, 92.1
POSSESSIVES: SNC 82, 83; IH 37.2, 57.2c, 67.4, 67.5, 82.2a, 82.5, 92.2; PES 6.3, 14.2
POSTPONED QUESTIONS, IH 52.7
PREDICATE ADJECTIVES, SNC 72
PREDICATE NOUNS, SNC 72
PREPOSITIONS: SNC 49, 70, 71, 84, 94, 95; IH 22.6i; 32.1, 37.6, 42.2, 42.3, 52.1, 56.2c, d, f, 57.1, 72.2, 76.7, 77.4h, 82.2a, 87.2; PES 7.4
pretty, IH 52.2
"PRE-VERBS," IH 82.3
PRONOUNS: SNC 23, 34, 34, 47, 48, 49, 49, 70, 82, 83, 96, 97; IH 12.1a, 12.4a, d, 17.2a, e, 17.3, 17.7, 22.4, 22.6, 22.8b, 22.9c, e, 32.1a, 37.2, 37.4, 42.5b, 46.4, 52.4b, 52.6f, 52.7d, 56.1, 57.2, 61.8, 67.5, 72.6, 82.5, Ap. 1; PES 1.1e, 6.3, 6.4, 7.4, 8.1a, 13.4, 14.3a
put, IH 51.1

QUESTIONS: SNC 24, 25, 33, 35, 84, 94; IH 12.4d, e, 17.1, 17.4c, 17.5d, 37.4d, 42.1c, 52.7; PES 2.1a, 2.2b, 3.2, 3.3, 4.1, 4.2b, 5.1, 5.4, 9.3, 12.2b, 12.3b, 13.1b, 17.1, 18.1

rarely, PES 5.3
ready, IH 81.9

report, IH 81.6
run: SNC 85; IH 37.7d

same, PES 15.1a, 15.1b
say: IH 52.6b, 66.7; PES 8.1a, 8.2c
see: SNC 91; PES 4.2a
seldom, PES 5.3
sell: SNC 84; IH 37.7b; PES 8.1b
send: SNC 73; IH 32.4b, 52.6b
SEPARABLE VERBS, See Composite Verbs
several, PES 14.3b
she: SNC 34; IH 17.3; PES 1.1e, 2.1c
shelf, IH 61.1
shine, IH 96.1
SHORT FORMS (See Contractions), IH 47.4a, 57.5
show, IH 52.6b
since, PES 18.1
so, IH 96.7
some: SNC 60, 68, 82; IH 27.1c, 31.1, 62.1, 77.2, 87.6a; PES 5.4, 6.1b
sometimes, PES 2.2a
sound, IH 66.5, 81.3
speak, PES 8.1a
spend: SNC 73; IH 32.4b
STATEMENTS: SNC 23; IH 12.1a, 12.1b; PES 1, 13.1a
still, PES 19.2
stop, IH 72.5a
STRESS, USE OF: SNC vii, 4, 5, 6, 8, 10, 15, 24, 46, 47, 48, 58, 59, 60, 69, 70, 71, 72, 82, 82, 84, 85, 91, 95, 96; IH xii, 2.7, 3.3, 3.7, 4.5, 5.8, 8.4, 8.5, 8.6, 8.7, 12.2, 12.4, 17.1a, 17.4b, 17.7b, 22.2a, 22.3a, 22.5b, c, 22.6, 22.9, 27.1a, 27.4c, 32.1a, d, 32.2a, 32.3, 37.1b, 37.2b, 37.5, 37.8, 42.3, 42.4a, 57.1, 57.7a, 62.1a, 62.2c, 62.5a, 67.2f, 70.1-6, 72.4c, 77.1a, 81.2, 82.1b, 87.6a
SUBJECT: SNC 23, 33, 34, 47, 49, 84; IH 12.1a, 12.1b, 17.1g, 22.7a, 22.8b, 47.3, 52.7d, 62.5, 67.2f, 72.5c, 72.6, 77.4e, 92.4b
SUBSTANTIVE EXPRESSIONS, IH 97.3
SUBSTITUTE SENTENCES: SNC 49, 50, 71; IH 22.8, 32.2, 62.2c; PES 1.1c, 2.1d, 3.4, 11.1c, 11.2a, 11.2b, 13.1d, 18.4
suppose, IH 62.2g

take, IH 56.5, 61.5, 61.6
teach, IH 81.1, 81.7
tell: SNC 91; IH 52.6b, 77.1a, 77.4e; PES 8.1b
than, IH 87.5a, 87.5f
that: SNC 47; IH 22.5, 77.1, 81.5; PES 6.3, 16.1, 17.2
the, PES 6.2, 15.1a, 15.3
them: SNC 48; IH 22.6e; PES 13.4
then, IH 62.6
there: IH 42.5a, 62.5; PES 14.1b
these: SNC 83; IH 37.3; PES 6.3
they: SNC 47; IH 22.4; PES 1.1b
think, IH 51.1
this: SNC 47; IH 22.5; PES 6.3
those: SNC 83; IH 37.3; PES 6.3
till, IH 87.4c
TIME-TELLING, IH 67.1, 72.1, 57.3b, 77.4d

to (prep.): SNC 94; IH 42.2a, 52.6d, 62.2a, 81.6, 86.2; PES 8.1a, 8.1b

too: SNC 24, 34, 35, 71; IH 12.2b, 17.2f, 32.2a; PES 13.3

tooth, IH 61.1

"TRANSITION FORMS," IH 82.4, 87.6c

true, IH 81.10

TWO-WORD VERBS, See composite verbs

understand: IH 32.4c; PES 4.2a

United States, IH 86.4

unpack, IH 51.2

until, IH 87.4c

up, IH 56.9, 61.4, 71.1, 96.2

us: IH 22.6d; PES 13.4

used to, PES 19.4

usually: IH 82.3b; PES 2.2a

VERBS: SNC 24, 24, 35, 36, 36, 49, 61, 62, 62, 72, 73, 80, 84, 85, 91, 94, 95, 97, 102, 104, *104f*; IH 12.2, 12.4, 17.4, 17.5, 17.6, 22.4b, 22.7, 22.8b, c, d, 22.9, 27.2, 27.3, 27.4, 32.2b, 32.4, 36.1, 37.7, 41.1, 41.6, 42.1, 42.2c, 42.3, 42.5b, 42.6b, 46.2, 47.1, 47.2, 51.1, 51.6, 52.4, 52.5, 52.6, 52.7, 52.8, 57.5, 62.3, 72.5, 77.1b, 77.4, 97.2, Ap. 5; PES 1.1b, 2.1a, b, c, 3.2, 3.3, 8.1a, 8.1c, 13.1, 18.1, 18.2, 18.5, 19.1, 19.4

VERBAL PHRASES: IH 47.3, 52.4a, 57.5, 57.6, 62.4a, 67.3, 72.3, 82.1, 92.5; PES 2.1a, b, c, 3.3, 4.2a, 5.1, 18.1, 2, 3, 4,11.1

very: IH 52.2, 67.2h; PES 13.3

wait, IH 81.5

wake, IH 61.4

want: IH 62.2a, 77.4e; PES 4.2a, 13.4

way, IH 77.4d, 82.4

well, IH 82.4, 87.5e

what: SNC 33; IH 17.1, 57.3b; PES 4.1, 4.2b, 5.1, 9.3

when: IH 57.3a, 87.4a; PES 4.1, 5.1, 9.3, 16.2a

where: SNC 33; IH 17.1; PES 4.1, 4.2b, 9.3

which: SNC 33; IH 17.1; PES 9.3

while, PES 16.2a

who: IH 57.2; PES 4.1, 4.2b, 5.1, 9.3

whole, IH 96.6

whom: IH 57.2b; PES 4.1

whose: IH 57.2c; PES 14.3a

why: IH 87.3; PES 12.2b

will: SNC 35, 73; IH 17.5c, 46.4, 52.4, 67.6

with: SNC 49, 71; IH 22.6, 32.1c

WORD ORDER: SNC 24, 25, 33, 46, 72, 82, 84, 96, 97, 97; IH 12.1b, 12.2, 12.5, 17.1a, f, g, 17.2g, 17.4a, c, 22.3a, 32.3, 37.2c, 37.4d, 42.3, 42.5, 42.7b, 47.3, 52.3, 52.6f, 57.2a, b, 57.3, 57.6a, b, 57.7b, c, 62.5a, d, 62.6, 77.4g, 82.1, 82.3; PES 1.1a, 2.1a, 2.2a, 2.2b, 3.1, 3.2, 4.1, 4.2b, 4.3, 5.1, 7.4, 8.1a, b, 9.1a, 9.3, 11.1a, 12.1, 13.4, 16.1, 17.1, 18.1, 19.2

would, IH 67.6

yet: IH 57.6; PES 19.2

you: SNC 24, 36, 48, 84; IH 12.3, 17.7, 22.6f, 37.5, 56.1, 67.3b; PES 13.4, 7.1

checked for Markings - 2-15-88 - clean

5-6-88